WarriorRage Kick-Boxing
Volume II

The Bolinger Boxing and Kick-Boxing program

Instructions in level 1 – 4 boxing, coaches mitts, medicine ball, heavy bag, both boxing and kickboxing drills.

Author: Scott Bolinger
WRKF Heavy Weight Champ

Copyright Feb. 2008 by
Scott Bolinger of Bolinger Kick-Boxing and Boxing
Alliance Nebraska

Disclaimer

The publisher and author of this instruction book and/or CD are not responsible in any manner whatsoever for any injury that may occur by reading and/or following any of the training activities whether it be physical or otherwise. It is advisable that before you start a training program to have approval from your physician so you have a professional opinion of whether or not you are capable of putting yourself through the rigorous training program.

Warning

I (Scott Bolinger) wrote this book for the beginner up to the coaches' level. This would include fighting techniques and different training programs. I however will not guarantee that the techniques described or illustrated in this book or CD will be safe or effective in any self-defense situation or otherwise. You may be injured if you apply or train with the techniques illustrated in this book and/or CD. To minimize the possibility of injury you should train with a professional and you should consult a physician before attempting to try anything in this book or CD. Scott Bolinger does not make any representation or warranty regarding the legality of appropriateness of any techniques. I will not guarantee your safety or guarantee that these techniques to be safe or beneficial to you.

Written by:
Scott Bolinger

Email: LB@LarryBolinger.com
Website: www.ScottBolinger.website

Context

Introduction

Scott Bolinger is the founder of the Warrior Rage Kickboxing Style and the author of this book. I'll start off this book with an introduction of myself, and my experiences, and hopefully, you'll have a better understanding of what it takes to be a successful fighter and/or coach whether it be for karate, tae kwon do, kickboxing, boxing, MMA or just to enhancing other sports by creating tone, flexibility and good hand/eye coordination. A lot of the explanations or examples in this book are in the fashion of a coach talking to a student.

While I was growing up, as a kid I did have many interests in different sports. My first sport was baseball and gymnastics. About 7th grade I got into weight lifting. My father who was the 1965 Mr. Nebraska taught me the proper way to lift weights. Then 8th and 9th grade I participated in wrestling. I started using martial arts weapons when I was 15. Mainly messing around with throwing stars and nunchakus. But I didn't get enrolled in a martial arts school until I was 16 years old. And martial arts came very naturally to me. With the combination of weight lifting and martial arts, it made me a faster and more powerful fighter. I was able to see a punch beginning to happen and pop up a sidekick or roundhouse kick faster than most people can throw a punch. The first art I studied was Shotokan Karate. I studied that for about 7 months, then went to just training myself for quite a while. I also studied Taekwon-Do, Kenpo, Jukaido, Boxing, and Chinese KickBoxing at various schools. But my primary art was always Shotokan.

I started competing in point tournament fights after I received my orange belt in Shotokan. I did try a few tournaments competing with weapons, kata, and Kumite, but I just found for myself that Kumite was my expertise. I was more comfortable with kumite because I was able to be zoned out so the crowd never bothered me, but when I did weapons or form I was always a little nervous.

One of the things that helped me in my fighting skills is that I had 5 buddies that I always trained and sparred with about every day. I believe in your development as a fighter, having one or more training partners would be a big help. That way you are not just doing the standard 2-day workout per week. To be better than the best, you have to go above and beyond your standard workout.

In 1987 I won the Paha Sapa Championships. Back then was a pretty big tournament. Also in 1987, I went on to win an open Tae Kwan Do tournament in Scottsbluff, then shortly after that I joined the Airforce and spent some time in Germany and competed in a few tournaments there. When I competed in Germany, that was the first time I ever lost a match. I lost 2 matches over there. But it was in 1988 that I eventually started writing this book. Jotting down what I learned, and what extra training I did to make me such a good fighter. Basically going threw my personal inventory of what I did to become a good fighter and what I was missing in my training then and worked on getting back on track. And also I would have a reference guide to fall back on so I didn't forget training techniques. I was honorably discharged from the Air Force in 1990. Then I decide to do a "try-one" in the Army National Guards. After that, I got a job working at a manufacturing plant, which was pretty much a dead-end job for about 9 years. In that time frame, I hardly ever trained.

In the year 2000, I had a change in jobs and started working for the YMCA. At that time I started back into training regularly as well as getting back to writing in my book. Working at the YMCA, I supervised basketball and volleyball. I started getting into shape again and eventually took on a couple of students to train in karate. With the extra time on my hands, I also diversified some income investing into stocks and rental property. The rental property did all right for a couple of years. It created the extra income to support some of my training needs. The stocks, most of them did so badly that I'd rather not talk about that..lol… But sometimes you gotta have a sense of humor about investments.

In 2002 I expanded my training and made my training sessions more open rather than just personal training. That kicked up my students to about 20 kids. And at that time we were training out doors. So when it started getting into winter I had to shut down. Having to do that, I started my quest to learn how to start up a Boxing and Kickboxing school. And also to learn how to raise money to buy a building. I weighed the different business filing on whether to file for for-profit or non-profit. I finally decided to go with the non-profit organization and got my non-profit status in Dec 2002 and reopened to start training in January 2003 and created the boxing and kickboxing school called the "Warrior Rage Civic Center," with my style of fighting called "Warrior Rage KickBoxing". During that break time, I also structured the katas to fit my own personal style of fighting. As a rule of thumb, practicing your katas on a daily basis will create better focus and enhance your fighting ability. Through a persistent effort, I found someone to donate the use of there building and I also took on 2 volunteer boxing coaches and we set up a training schedule for the boxers and kickboxers. At that time I found a pretty big interest in boxing techniques and training and started incorporating that into my kickboxing style and it worked extremely well. And I got a real kick out of seeing my fighters change, and grow into mature respectable fighters.

Looking back at the two losses in German, I guess I'm still a little pissed about that. But I also think, if I hadn't had those losses, that maybe I wouldn't have written this book and maybe I wouldn't of grown into such a good coach. But, I'm not saying I wouldn't mind competing against those guys again. I wouldn't mind that at all.

The school I ran on 1st in Box Butte in Alliance Nebraska ran for about 6 or 7 months, and then I closed it down do to, the owner of the building wasn't someone I'd have associated with the kids I trained. But, I continued training out of my home, then in January 2003, opened up a gym in Chadron with some help from Joe Simmons, who also runs the Native American Center in Chadron. I met him when I was on the board of a youth club and campaigning for a City Council spot. At close to the same time frame I expanded the school and started teaching at the Pine Ridge Job Corps. Ran that for about a year, then when the Job Corps changed the athletics coordinator position, they got rid of the boxing program. I then moved to 507 Niobrara in Alliance and from there, I was able to set up a better training program there. So the business started expanding well there and I set up a website at www.warriorrage.com to help with promotions and keep track of events. MMA was growing quickly and I started getting requests to help fighters get ready to compete in MMA, so I jumped in on that and started training MMA athletes, mainly helping with their stand-up game.

In August 2006 I started up a KickBoxing federation called the "WarriorRage KickBoxing Federation" and had my first fight under the WRKF rules in February 2007 in McCook, NE. I did an exhibition match against Matt Golding who later that year took 1st in the Cornhusker state games. The style of competition that I wrote up for the WRKF is set up as a continuous point sparring competition. Would be similar to international rules, but as a point-based system. I expanded another website that described in detail of my federation and It covers the rules and regulations at www.wrkf.us. I worked on that for several years to get it nationally recognized.

The new place at 507 Niobrara in Alliance is a 8 bedroom home, which gives me enough space to devote rooms for a weight lifting room, bag room, and sparring room as well as able to rent rooms out to athletes that want to live at my facility and training every day. This is good for people who want to step up their game and create a future in combat sports. I expand on WRKF products, having available: sparring equipment, weapons, shirts, and hoodies. I then added an artist to the payroll to help with the designs and then added the ability to help other coaches create their own training manual or book. To help give them the chance to get their books published at a reasonable price. In 2008 I changed the name of my fighting style to Bolinger Kick-Boxing and Bolinger Boxing.

In 2008 I started having requests to sanction some pro-am fights for Muay Thai, boxing, and MMA. So that gave me some incentive to create a third book on rules and regulations and expand my official's training program. In the officials training program, I go over rules and regulations for whatever competition we're doing, then go through a self-defense course. I made it a requirement that both security personnel and officials take the course. The self-defense course I was teaching was to teach different defensive moves and restraints that didn't consist of any strikes. So if someone got out of hand, everyone would be on the same page and would know what to do and how to help each other. But I had my training programs open to the law enforcement as well. A lot of the self-defense moves I was teaching are widely taught in different human services programs.

One thing my Granddad always said is that if you stay persistent and consistent in your efforts eventually things will come together. That is a bit of advice I've always lived by. Things don't grow overnight. Stay persistent and consistent and eventually you'll have a profitable business.

How to use this Book

The way I teach both kickboxing and boxing, I have set up test levels for each art, having the combination of technique training, as well as conditioning. In my boxing style, I do 4 testing levels, having the combination of a medicine ball routine and mitt work. For the first 4 chapters, there will be the routine for that test level and a page number of where to locate that exercise. After the routine, there will be pictures of how to execute each exercise.

My suggestion for the training is, to start off with Level 1 and stay with that training for at least a month before moving on to Level 2. Level 2, would be at least 2 months long to be able to obtain good tone. Then if you have a training partner, I'd jump to level 4 on the medicine ball, then to level 3. The Level 3 medicine ball routine is the hardest and you gotta be fairly well toned to be able to do that exercise. If you're comfortable with the level 2 medicine ball, then jump right in on the level 3. Then you can go through the level 2 medicine ball routine every other day, and then on your off days, go through the level 3 medicine ball. If you don't have a medicine ball or dumbbells, a lot of people make up some sandbags. If you do this I'd suggest making a couple of 5 lbs, 10, 13, and 16 lbs sand bags. If you plan on teaching a large group, this would be a cheap way to obtain equipment to teach a large class without buying 20 or 30 medicine balls.

With the heavy bag routines, I'd start off with the first routine for a couple of weeks before moving on to the second. When you have students working on the heavy bag, it's a little easier to teach proper torque for your hooks and uppercuts. There are a few ways to work the heavy bag, one is by doing the routines that are listed in here, and the other is free style it and mix up your combo. Something similar to shadowboxing. Both are good to practice.

Special Thanks:

To my students who helped me put together this book: Lance Yearling, Victor Camacho (2008 Central State Light Heavy Weight Champ), Rey Zuniga (placed 2nd in state for Tae-Kwon-Do 2006 and #2 in MMA (sponsored by Championship Boxing and Who's Your Daddy promotions) as a light Heavy Weight and place 1st in state for Tae Kwon Do in 2008, #1 in WRKF MMA heavyweight. And my Cousin and student Aaron Morris students Erick Rippe and Bryce Adamson.

Chapter 1
Punches and Strikes

Aaron Morris

On a standard punch, jab, or cross punch, you use the forefinger and middle finger knuckle as your striking knuckles. Try and get in the practice that if your jab is out, your rear hand is by your cheek and if your rear hand is out, your lead hand is by your cheek.

Jab – A jab comes from the leading hand and shoots straight out.

Cross – A cross punch comes from the trailing hand. You torque your hips and also pivot on the ball of your trailing foot.

Vertical punch – you strike with the forefinger knuckle and middle finger knuckle. You throw it like you are starting a jab or cross, but you keep your hand vertical instead of twisting your hand.

Backfist strike – you hit with the back of the middle finger knuckle and forefinger knuckle. You may also use the full back of the hand. In boxing, you'll only be able to hit with the knuckle part. If you have an amateur boxing competition glove, that striking area would be the white part of the glove In most kickboxing, you can use the full back of the hand.

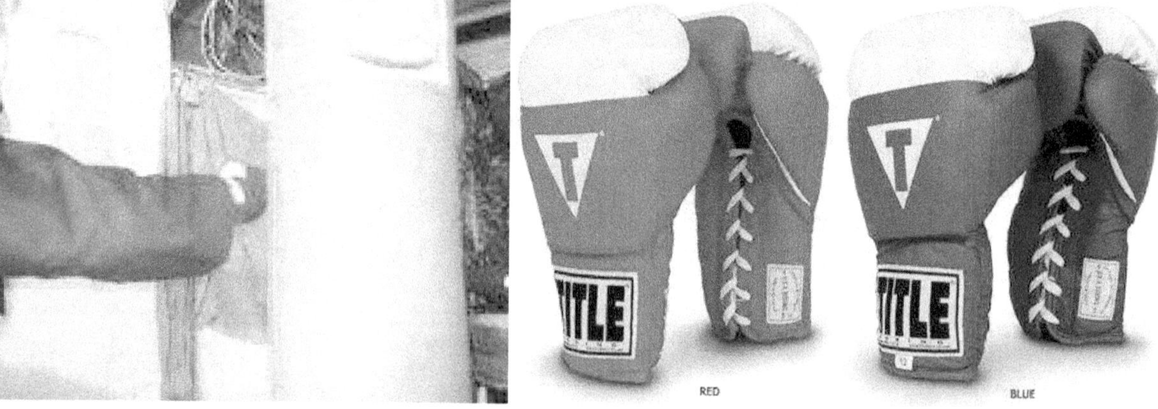

throwing a back fist, you lift your elbow up and then throw your fist out to the side of your target.

Spinning Back-Fist: When throwing a spinning technique, you want to see your target before you throw your strike and that'll be a split second later. When turning, you cross your arms in the middle of your spin to get full extension of your back fist, creating a stronger strike.

Spinning Step Threw Back fist
With a spinning step threw back-fist, in the example in a right stance you turn counterclockwise and when you turn you're also stepping your foot around and crossing your arms to get full extension of your back fist. Note, usually a step through back fist is a strike after a kick, which will be shown below.

Reverse front kick, jab, step through spinning back fist:

Hook Punch – hitting with the forefinger knuckle and middle finger knuckle. Punching to the midsection your fist is vertical, punching to the head your fist is horizontal. To get more power in your hook, you don't want to be too far from your opponent. If you have to reach to hit your target, you take away your power. You should be close enough to be able to torque your hips into the punch.

Reverse Hook Punch

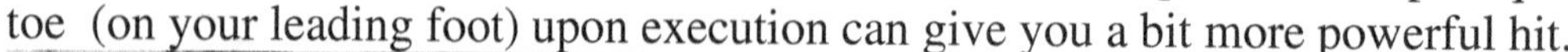

Uppercut Punch – a little dip and come from underneath, put a little hip torque, and raise up on your toe (on your leading foot) upon execution can give you a bit more powerful hit.

Reverse Uppercut

Chapter 2
Kicks

Side Kick – Raise your knee up and then kick to the side and hit with your heel bring the knee back and step down.

Spinning Side Kick: If you are standing in a stance where your right foot is forward, you turn counterclockwise. Turn your head first, then pick up your left leg and hit with your heel.

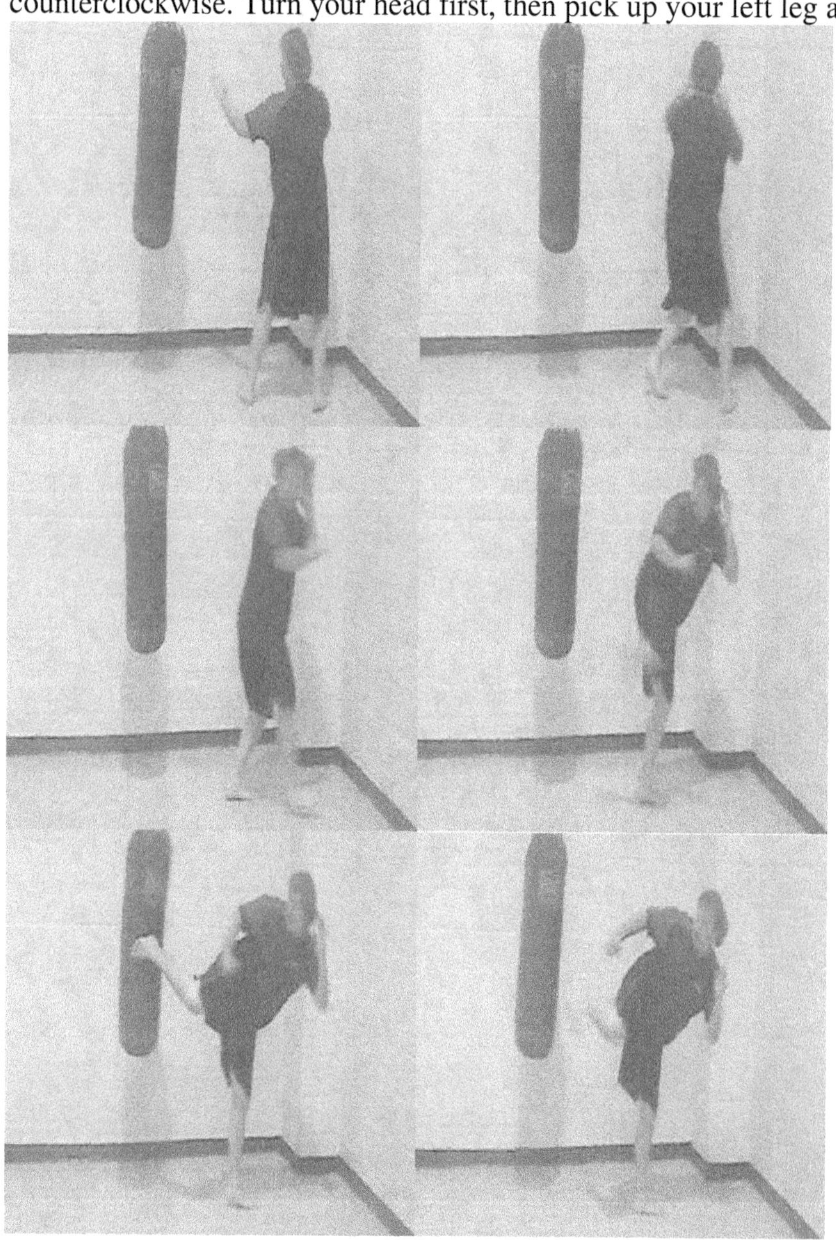

Front Kick Lift your knee up, extend your foot, and hit with the ball of your foot.

Knee up

Foot out hit will the ball of the foot, retract the foot.

Foot down, back in a ready stance.

Reverse Front Kick: A reverse comes from the back leg, you start in your ready stance, and you turn torque your hips then lift your knee up and execute your kick.

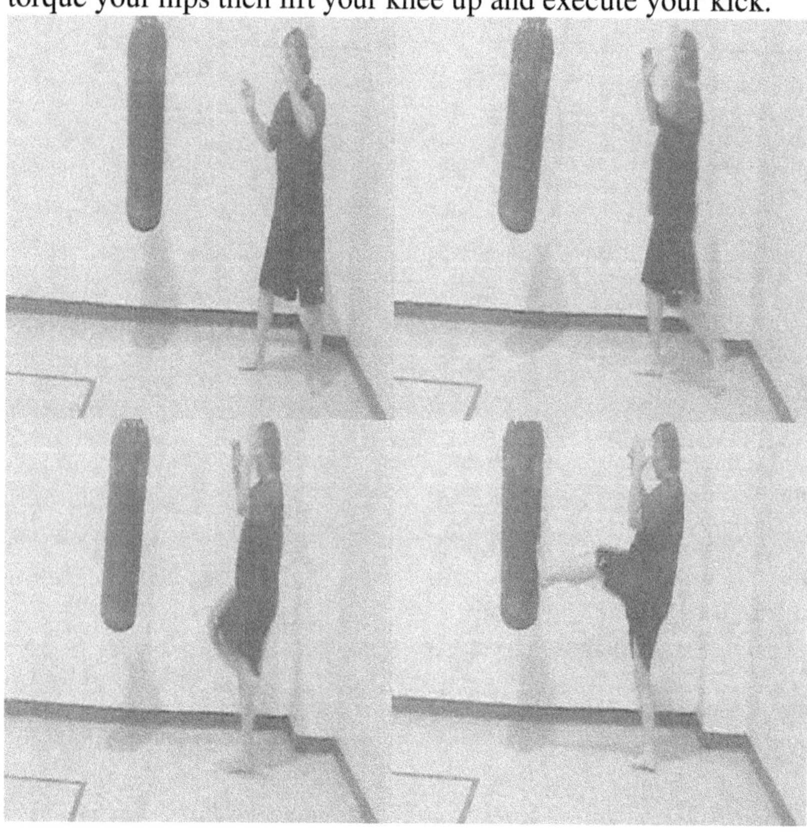

Round House Kick – with a roundhouse kick, you are kicking with the top of your foot (also called the instep). You bring the knee up, throw the kick out, bring the foot back, and then step down.
(Note: You'll hit with the shin if attacking the thigh or midsection. You may hit with the top of the foot if attacking the midsection or head. On a thigh kick you'll usually chop down on the roundhouse kick and then attack at a slight angle upward when attacking the midsection to come up under the elbow.)

Bring the knee up, extend the foot, bring the foot back, and then down back to a ready stance.

Reverse Round-House kick: a reverse roundhouse will come from the trailing leg, you pivot your up[per] body, torque your hips around lift your leg, and kick in a fluent motion. If you are kicking low like in [the] pictures below, that would be a kick to the thigh. With a kick to the thigh, you would angle your kick downward and you would strike the thigh with your shin. If you kick to the midsection, the ideal spot [to] strike to the midsection would be the second rib up and usually on the right side of the body either str[ike] with the shin or instep. But if kicking to the midsection your kick would be slightly angled upward to come up under an elbow.

Hook Kick: On a hook kick, you through it like a sloppy sidekick, then you hook your foot back, so y[ou] hit with your heel or ball of the foot.

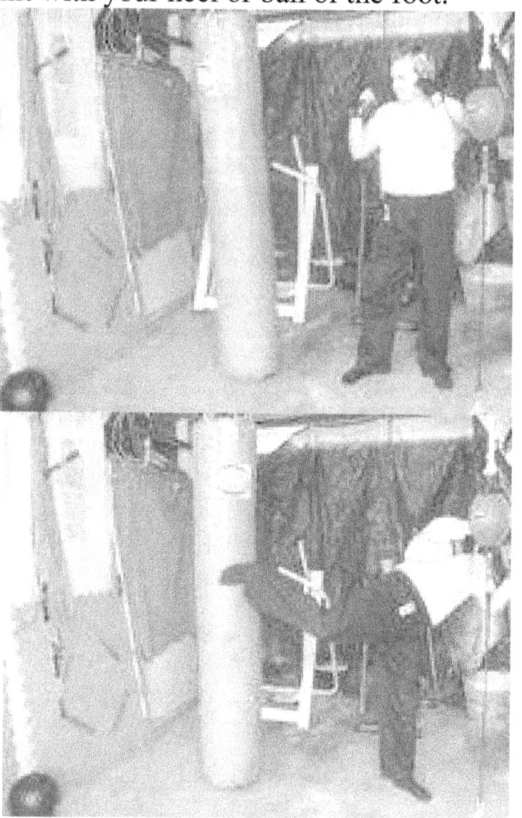
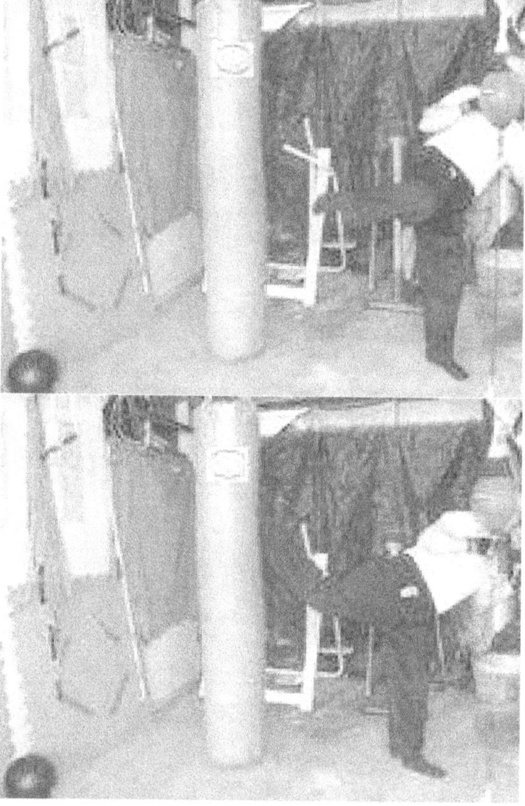

Close up on Hook Kick:

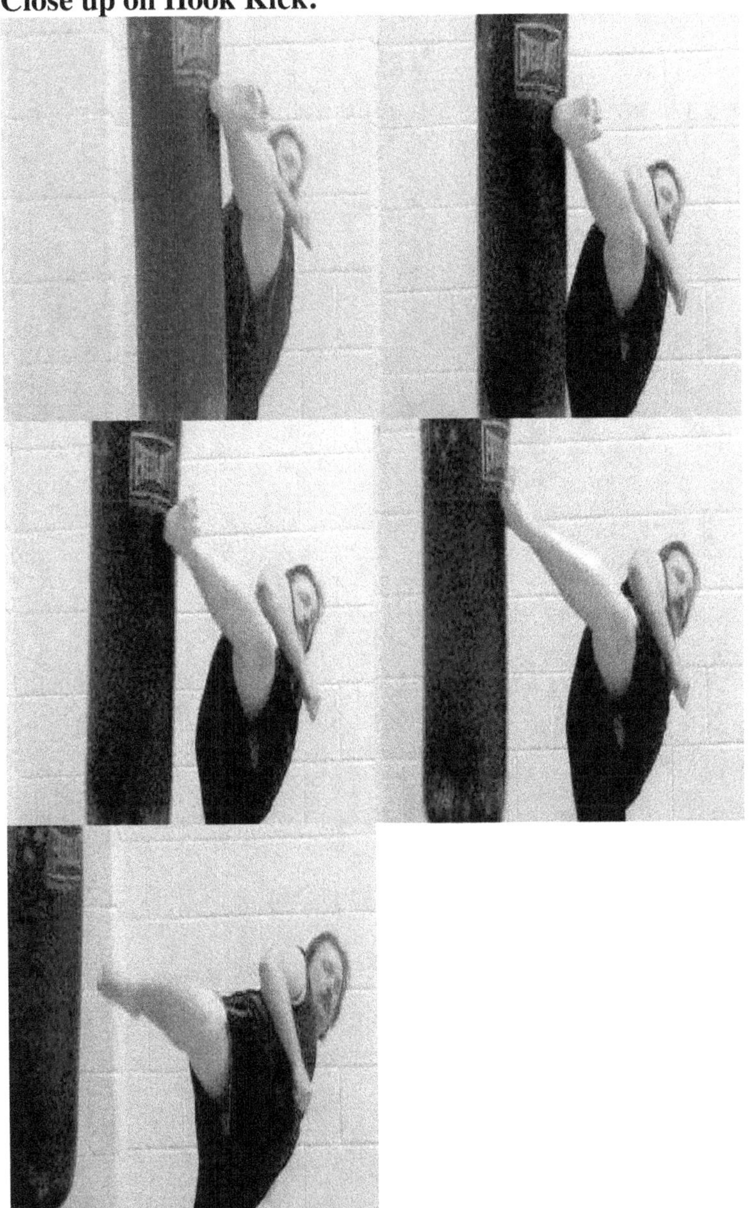

The difference between a step-up technique and a pick-up technique

Pick-up Side Kick: Pick up the knee throw the side kick, hit with the heel of the foot, pull the leg back, and then drop the foot down.

Step up Side Kick: Start from your ready stance, move the left foot towards the right foot and touch heel to heel, pick up the right knee, execute a side kick, pull your knee back, put your right foot down right beside your left heel, then move your left foot back. Now you are back to where you began (in your ready stance).

Half step: an example is shown in a common combination.
Jab, half step, Jab, cross: Jab, then step your leading foot forward in a half-step (about 8 to 10 inches) then bring your trailing leg up (the trailing foot will be on the ball of the foot), execute a jab, cross combination. Then, move your trailing leg back, then your leading leg back. Now you are back in the same exact position you started in.

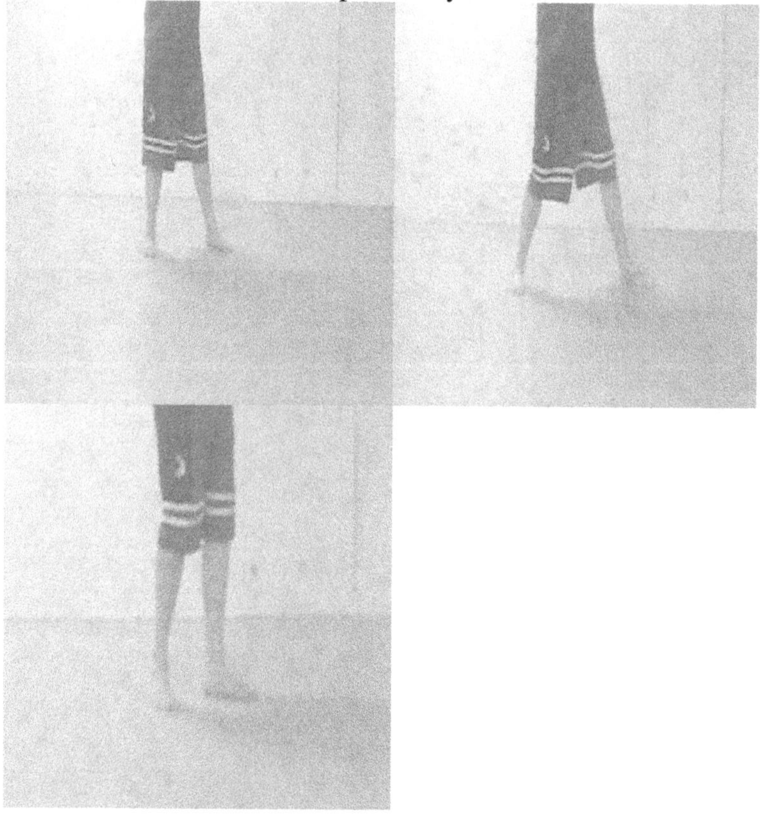

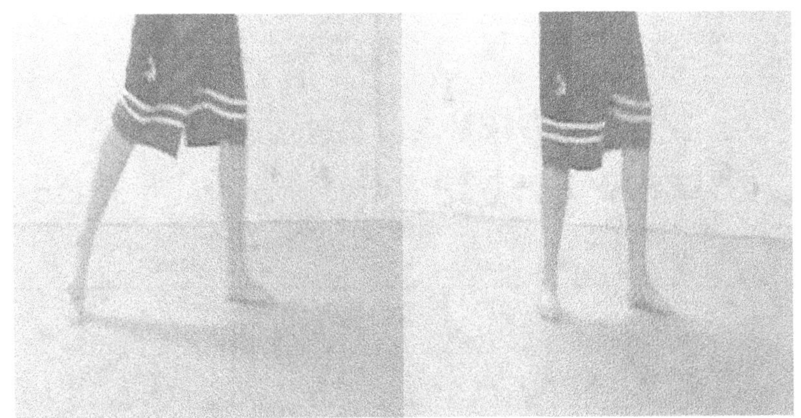

Chapter 3
Stripe Test Level 1

Lance Yearling

<u>Warm-up exercise for level 1</u>
Run a mile or 2X2 minute rounds on the jump rope, and work your way up to 2 miles or 3X2 minute rounds on the jump rope. *Note: when jogging long distances you'll need to get to work on a breathing technique. Either one long breath out and two short breaths in or one long breath in and two short breaths out usually works well)*

20 - sit-ups (pg. 30)
10 - 20 - sit-ups right elbow to left knee (pg. 30)
10 – 20 - sit-ups left elbow to right knee (pg 30)
20 – kick-outs (pg. 30)
10 – figure 8 (pg. 31)
10 – circles (pg. 31)
10 – side leg lifts (pg. 31)
10 – Bench Press (32)
10 – Pullovers (32)
Note: with the Bench press and pullovers, start with a set of 10 and work your way up to 3 sets of 10
10 – shoulder rotations (32)
10 – Side Crunches (pg. 35)
10 – side lats (pg. 33)
10 – overhead raise (33)
10 – 2 handed overhead (pg. 34)
10 – Curl (pg. 36)
10 – press (33)
10 – French curl (pg. 37)
10 – underhand press (34)
Note: with the curl, press, French curl, and underhand press, start off with one set of 10 and work your way up to 3 sets of 10
10 - sit-ups – chest to toes (pg. 35)
10 – sit-ups – chest to knee (pg. 35)
10 – sit-ups – straight arm sit-ups (pg. 36)
10 – sit twist (pg. 36)
Coaches Mitts Level 1
Punch your left glove to your coach's left mitt and your right glove to your coach's right mitt.
<u>Round 1 level 1</u>
10 jab, cross, jab (pg. 37)
10 jab, cross, hook (pg. 38)
10 jab, cross, hook, reverse hook (pg. 39)
10 jab, cross, duck, jab, cross (pg. 39)
10 jab, cross, uppercut, reverse uppercut, jab cross (pg 40)

<u>Round 2 level 1</u>
Practice 2-step combo (pg. 41)
1st Combination: When 2 gloves are up execute a jab, cross, jab
2nd Combination: When 1 glove is up, execute a jab, then step up and do a jab, cross

Practice 3-step combo (pg. 45)
1st Combination: When 2 gloves are up, execute a jab, jab, cr
2nd Combination: When 1 glove is up, execute a jab, if the glove goes sideways, execute a leading hand hook (pg.
3rd Combination: When 1 glove is up, execute a jab, if the other hand goes up and both gloves go sideways, then execute a leading hand hook, reverse hook, and a leading hand hook

Medicine Ball Exercises Level 1

Sit-ups

Sit-ups right elbow to left knee switch legs around for left elbow to right knee (it may be helpful to have a training partner hold down your leg)

Kick-Outs – almost like a bicycle, but you are kicking the heal out

Figure 8 (hold your feet 4 to 8 inches off the ground and move them in a Figure 8)

Circles -- similar to figure 8, but you move your feet in a circle, usually 5 to 10 clockwise, then 5 to 10 counter clock-wise)

Side Leg lift

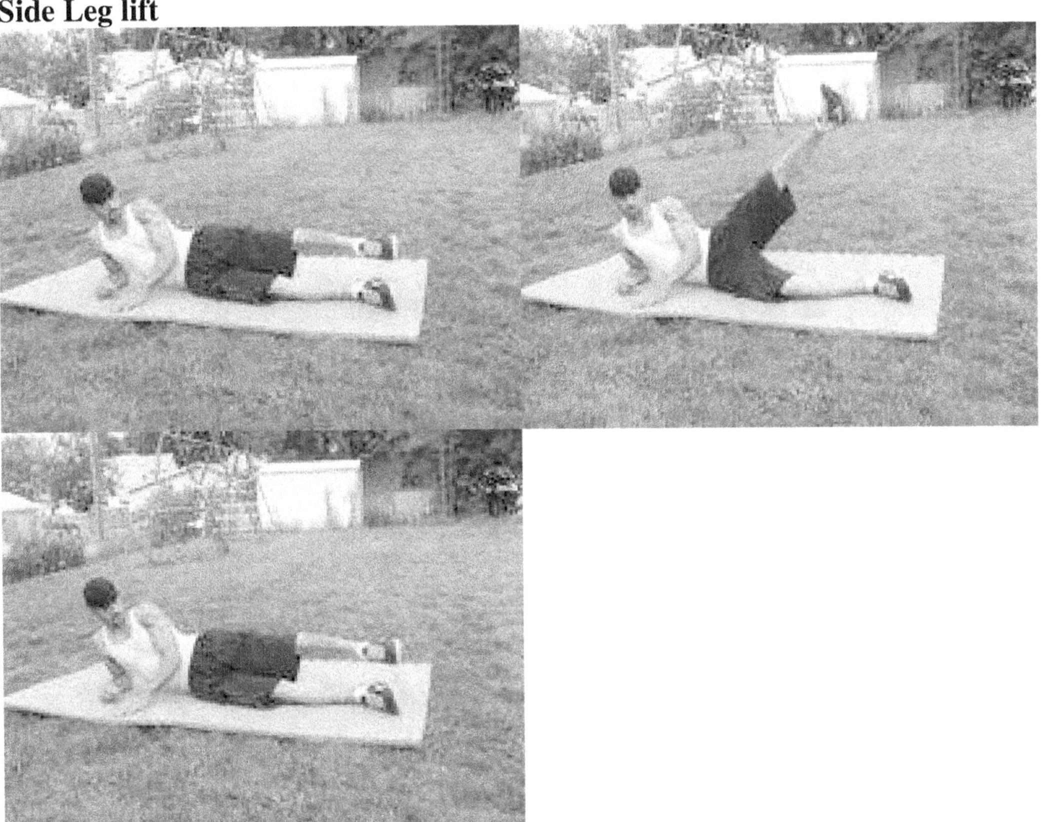

Bench Press

Pullovers

Shoulder Rotations (rest your elbow on your side and rotate your shoulder forward and back)

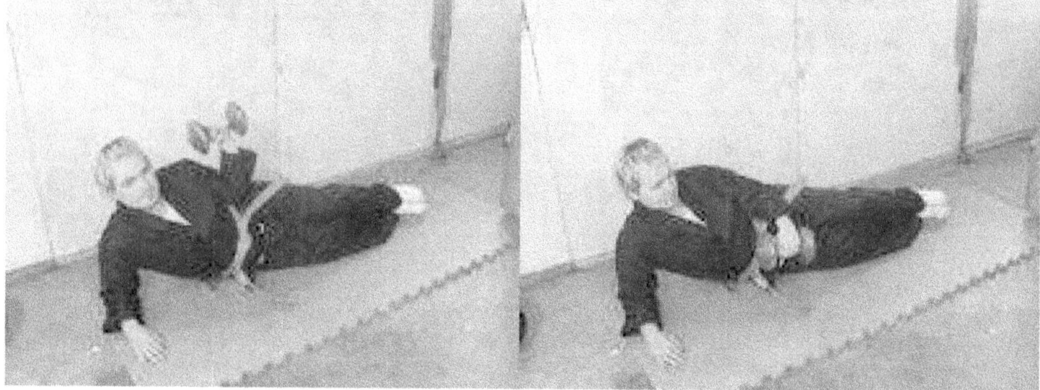

Side lats – in this exercise, you will need between a 2 to 10-pound weight in your hand, start with your hand up high, and when you bring your hand down you also move your chest to face the ground to get a good pull.

Over-Head Raise

Press

Underhand press: Your hands are underneath the medicine ball and you press up

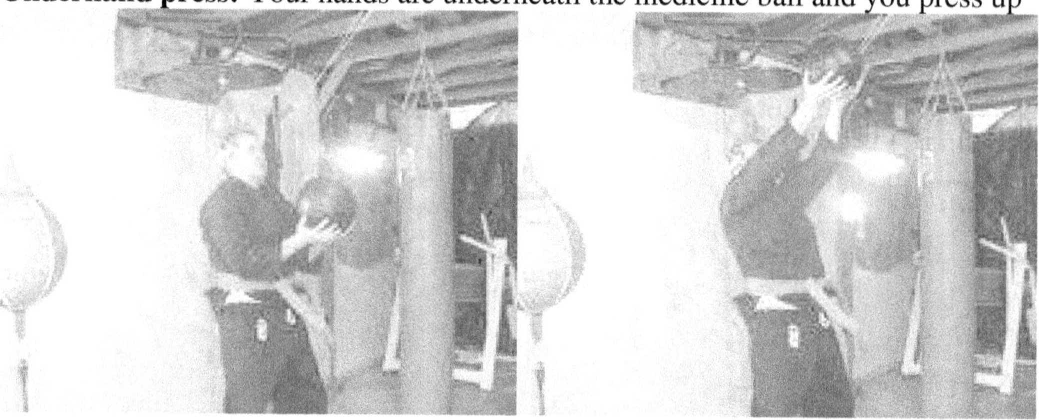

Two-handed overhead

Side crunches – bring up your knee and at the same time bring down your elbow. When doing this, focus on the side muscles and tighten your side muscles when bringing your elbow down and your knee up.

Sit-up – chest to toes (when pushing the medicine ball up to the toes you should be lifting your shoulders a few inches off the ground)

Sit-ups – chest to knee (with this sit-up you'll be about halfway up, not quite a full sit-up)

Sit-ups – straight arm sit-ups (with this sit-up, you are coming up all the way into a full sit-up position)

Sit Twist: when performing this exercise you touch the ball to the ground

Curls

French Curl

Coaches Mitts Level 1

Note: *Most of the time, when I'm working the coach's mitts, I have my student hit the gloves having the left hand hit the left mitt and the right glove hitting the right mitt. Do not stay in one position. Move in a circle as if you were sparring.*

Jab, Cross, Jab – a lot of times the cross is also referred to as a straight punch or straight reverse. Take note of when executing the cross, the torque of the hips and pivot on the ball of the foot

Jab, Cross, Hook – it's good practice to practice the hook to the head as well as to the body. The belly guard is a great help in working the body shots. When hooking to the body, try and get your student to use hip torque.

Jab, Cross, Hook, Reverse hook

Jab, Cross, Duck, Jab, Cross (when working this combination, the coach should switch back and forth from throwing a jab or a cross and make sure that the student isn't looking down. His eyes should be focused on the coach, usually looking at the chest. Focusing on the chest, you can see every movement so you'll be able to react to that)

Jab, Cross, Uppercut, Reverse Uppercut, Jab, Cross – this is a good speed drill. This isn't a power drill, just focus on speed.

Practice 2 step combo
1st combination: When the coach has 2 mitts up the students execute a jab, cross, jab
2nd combination: When the coach has 1 mitt up, execute a jab, then step up and do a jab, cross
(when working a 2-step combination, you are working two sets of combinations. Mix it up, back
and forth of having one hand up or two hands)

1st Combination: when the coach puts up 2 mitts – the student executes a jab, cross, jab

2nd Combination: When the coach puts up one mitt – the student executes a jab, then steps up, jab, cross

▶ The coach puts up one hand, the student throws a Jab

▶ the student brings his hand back, then the coach evades back

▶ The student steps forward with his lead foot, step up about 6 to 8 inches. The instant you land your second jab, your foot should be stepping down. This will make the second jab have a lot more power, having your weight flowing with your punch.

▶ When executing your cross, you also bring up your rear foot up about 6 to 8 inches. Notice the heal off the ground. If you don't bring up the foot, you may end up over-extending your punch. When you do that, the return of your punch may be longer or slower and easier to counter. So it is a must to bring up the rear foot so you don't over-extend.

▶ Step the rear foot back, then step the leading foot back, now you are back in your starting position.

Practice 3-step combo (in a 3-step combo, you are working 3 combos at the same time)
1st Combination: When the coach puts up 2 mitts, the student executes a jab, jab, cross
2nd Combination: When the coach puts up 1 mitt the student executes a jab, if the mitt goes sideways the student executes a leading hand hook
3rd Combination: When the coach puts up 1 mitt the student executes a jab, if the other hand goes up and both mitts go sideways, then the student follows up the combination with a leading hand hook, reverse hook, and a leading hand hook

1st Combination: When the coach puts up two mitts, then the student executes a jab, jab, cross

2nd Combination: When the coach puts up one mitt the student executes a jab, if that same mitt goes sideways, the student executes a leading hand hook

► With this particular combination, right after you execute the hook, you step the back foot around. When stepping around, you want to keep the same distance between you and your opponent. If you close the gap when stepping around, you could put yourself in a position to be countered. This combination was designed as if you were up against the ropes, your opponent advances, you jam him with a jab, and if he walks through that, you hook him in the side of the head and move, getting off the ropes. Hopefully with a hook, if you knock him off balance, you jump back in with a jab, jab, cross.

3rd Combination: When the coach puts up one mitt the student executes a jab, when the coach's mitt that's up goes sideways and the other coach's mitt comes up, then the student executes a leading hand hook, reverse hook, and a leading hand hook. Then step it around as shown above

Chapter 4
Stripe Test Level 2

Victor Camacho

<u>Level 2 Medicine ball routine</u>
20-sit-ups (pg. 30)
10 - sit-ups right elbow to left knee (pg. 30)
10 - sit-ups left elbow to right knee (pg. 30)
20- Kick-outs (pg. 30)
10 - figure 8 (pg. 31)
10 – circles (pg. 31)
10 – side leg lift (pg. 31)
10 – side lats (pg. (33)
10 – side crunches (pg. 35)
10 - sit-ups – chest to toes (pg. 35)
10 – sit-ups – chest to knee (pg. 35)
10 – sit-ups – straight arm sit-ups (pg. 36)
10 – sit and twist side to side (pg. 36)
10 to 20 pull-overs (pg. 51)
10 – 2 leg bridges (pg. 51)
10 – 1 leg bridge (pg. 51)
10 – push-ups – hit chest on the ball (pg. 52)
10 - push-ups – one hand on the ball and one on the ground, then switch hands and do another set of 10 (pg. 52)
10 – push-ups – both hands on the ball (pg. 52)
Note: at this time if you want to do more for the shoulders, you could add 3X10 or 3 sets of 10 on the bench press. After you are done with the bench press, finish up the rest of this routine)

Note: For the next four exercises you will do one right after the other. You will do a set of curls then move to a set of presses, then move to a set of French curls, then a set of underhanded presses. Repeat that 3 times to get 3X10 or 3 sets of 10)
3X10 – curls (pg. 53)
3X10 – Press (pg. 33)
3X10 – French curls (pg. 53)
3X10 – Underhanded press (pg. 34)

10 – shoulder flexion (pg. 53)
10 – Giant Circles (pg. 54)
10- Woodchopper (pg. 55)
10- squats – ball overhead (pg. 55)
10- Dip extensions (pg. 55)
10 – shoulder twist (pg. 56)
10 – stand up side twist (pg. 56)
10 to 20 – lateral bend – side to side (pg. 56)
10 to 20 – front to back – bend (pg. 57)
10 – squats – ball on chest (pg. 58)
10 – squats – ball on the neck (pg. 58)
10 – front lunges (pg. 58)
10 – back lunges (pg. 58)

10 – side lunge (pg. 59)
10 – one leg squat (pg. 59)

1-minute drills
jump over ball – side to side (pg. 60)
jab, jab, cross on the heavy bag (pg. 61)
jump over ball – front to back (pg. 61)
speed hooks on the heavy bag (pg. 62)

<u>Level 2 coaches mitts</u>

<u>Round 1 level 2</u>

practice blocks

20 palm blocks using the reverse hand against a jab (pg. 63)
20 palm blocks using the reverse hand against a cross (pg. 63)
20 Parry with the reverse hand against a jab (pg. 63)
20 Parry with the leading hand against a cross (pg. 64)
20 shoulder blocks also called shoulder shrug (pg. 64)

In the next two sets, I move around like we were sparring and go back and forth between throwing a jab and cross.
▶ Set of 10 -- coach throws a jab, student parries with the reverse hand, and counters with a leading hand hook to the body. (pg. 64)
▶ Set of 10 -- coach throws a cross, student parries with the leading hand, and counters with a reverse hook to the body. (pg. 64) .

Note: on the next two drills, I go back and forth between throwing the jab and the cross but I try and get 10 sets on each parry and counter combo or I go till the boxer or kick-boxer looks more comfortable with the combination.
▶ Set of 10 to 15 -- coach throws a jab, student parries with the reverse hand, counters with a leading hand hook to the body, leading hand hook to the head, reverse hook to the head. (pg. 65)
▶ Set of 10 to 15 -- coach throws a cross, student parries with the leading hand, counters with a reverse hook to the body, jab to the head, cross to the head. (pg. 66)

To work on defense against hooks you can use this substitute:
If you want to work on more defense and counters against hooks, you can substitute your defensive drill with this drill.
▶ 10 to 20 coach throws a hook, the student does a reverse back fist block and counters with a leading hand hook to the body If the coach throws a reverse hook, the student does a leading hand back fist block and then executes a reverse hook to the body.

Note: on the next two drills, I go back and forth between throwing the leading hand hook and the reverse hook but I try and get 10 sets on each counter combo

▶ The coach throws a leading hand hook to the head, the student does a reverse hand back fist block, counters with a leading hand hook to the body, leading hand hook to the head, reverse hook to the head.

▶ The coach throws a reverse hook, the student does a leading hand back fist block, counters with a reverse hook to the body, jab to the head, cross to the head.

Round 2, 3 and 4 Level 2
Intervals

Start with two sets at 2 minute long (also written as 2X2). As your endurance grows and you get used to the drill, increase the rounds and duration. The goal would be to do 3 rounds at 3 minutes long. Stand square to your coach and keep a steady pace. When you start to feel the stress, just breathe in through the nose and out through the mouth to help keep control of your breathing and at the same time keep the pace of your strikes.

30 seconds uppercuts, 30 seconds straight punches, 30 seconds uppercuts, 30 seconds straight punches. (pg. 68)

Intervals on a Heavy Bag: stand square to the bag, do straight punches, left, right, left, right for 30 seconds, then hooks (to the body) for 30 seconds, straight punches for 30 seconds, then another set of hooks for 30 seconds. You might start off with 2X2 minute rounds, but work your way up to 3X3 minute rounds.

Note: To help with your defense there are some sparring drills you can do. You can do one or two rounds of sparring where one person throws the punches and the other practices their blocks (palm blocks, parries, back fist blocks, elbow blocks, shoulder blocks, and evades). For kickboxers, you can do a round or two, just working the hands on this drill, but also do a round that you block with the hands and counter with the roundhouse to the thigh. On the kickboxing drill what you would usually do is parry with one hand and counter kick with the opposite leg. So if you are both standing with the left leg forward, if the coach throws a jab, the student would parry with the reverse hand, then counter with a reverse roundhouse kick to the outside of the leg. If the coach throws a cross, the student parries with the leading hand and then counters with a roundhouse kick to the inside of the thigh. Both kicks land on the leading leg of the coach.

Pull Overs – the starting position is straight above your head then bring your arms straight above you and back.

2 leg Bridge – both feet are on the ball, then bridge your hips up

One leg Bridge – one leg is on the ball, then bridge your hips upward

Push-ups – Hit chest on the ball – both hands are on the outside of the ball, when you go down you touch the ball on your chest, then back up to where your arms are straight.

Push-ups – one hand on the ball and one on the ground, then switch hands and do another set of 10

Push-ups – both hands on ball

Curls

French Curl

Shoulder Flexions – (keep arms straight through the entire movement)

Giant circles

Wood Choppers – The starting position is with the medicine ball At your shoulder then come straight down to your center and bend your knees (Common practices are to either chop a lot of wood or exercise by hitting a sludge hammer on an old tractor tire. *note: take the rim out of the tractor tire*)

Squats – Ball overhead

Dip Extensions

Shoulder Twist – with the shoulder twist you move the ball from side to side without moving the trunk.

Stand-up side twist – twisting side to side and in this exercise, you move the trunk.

Lateral Bend

Front to Back

Squats – Ball on Chest

Squat – Ball on the back of the neck

Front Lunge

Back Lunge

Side Lunge

One Leg Squat – you can perform this squad with a cinder block or off a stair step.

Minute Drills

In this exercise, what we'll do is we'll do a drill on a matt, jumping side to side, then go to the heavy bag, do the combo jab, jab, cross, then go back to the matt, jump front to back, then go back to the heavy bag and do a minute drill on hooks.

What I've done is take one of my puzzle mats and put some duct tape on it to know where to jump to. Once you get used to that, then put a medicine ball in the middle to force a higher jump.

Jump side to side

Heavy Bag – jab, jab, cross

Jump Front to Back

Heavy bag – speed hooks (on a speed hook, you put your head into the bag and throw hooks as fast as you can for a minute. You'll usually need someone to hold the bag for you on this drill.)

Mitt Work Level 2
Jab, Cross, Leading hand hook to the body, Leading hand hook to the head

Palm Block against a Jab (when practicing the palm block, the student needs to keep his/her chin down. The student is catching the coach's mitt in the palm of their hand. You keep the chin down, so if someone punches too hard, your glove will hit the top of your head, instead of your nose. And it's good practice to do because an easy knockout is done on people who have their chin too high.

Palm Block against a Cross

Parry the Jab (with this block, you are moving the strike, just past your cheek)
Note: Don't over-extend. If you overextend the block, that'll take you longer to return your hand, leaving your side open to a counter, or possibly putting you off balance

Parry the Cross

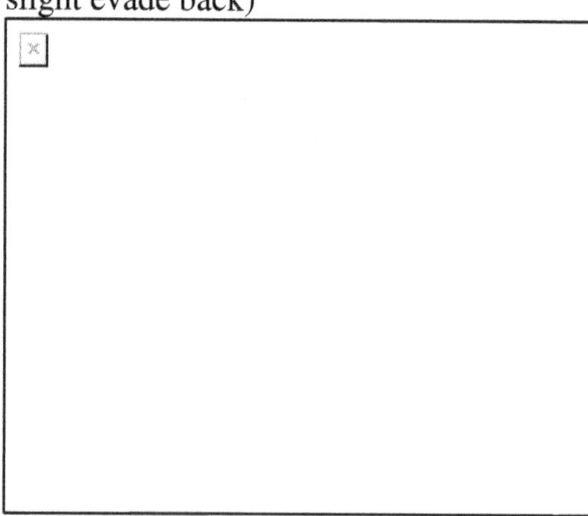

Shoulder Block or Shoulder Shrug (with a shoulder block, you shrug the shoulder up and do a slight evade back)

Reverse hand parry, lead hand hook to the body

Lead hand parry followed by the counter strike reverse hook to the body

Coach throws a Jab. The student parries with the reverse hand, counters with a leading hand hook to the body, then chambers his arm and executes a leading hook to the head then a reverse hook to the head.

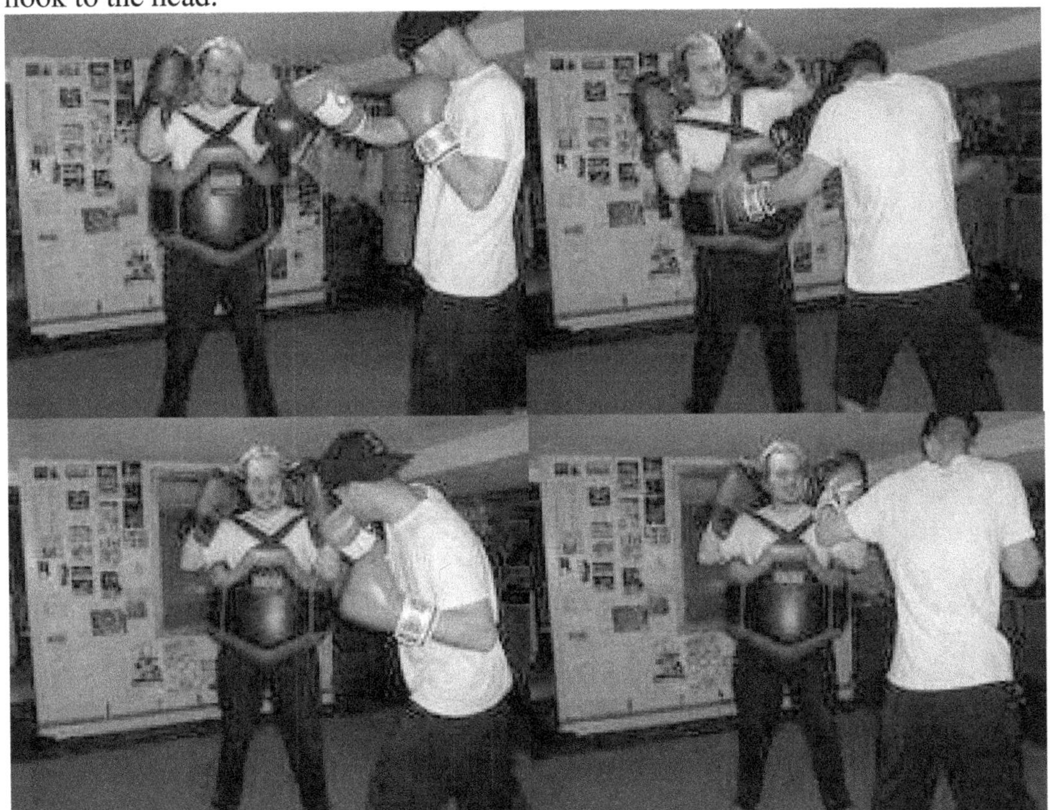

The coach throws a cross. The student parries the jab with a leading hand parry then counters with a reverse hook to the body, jab, cross

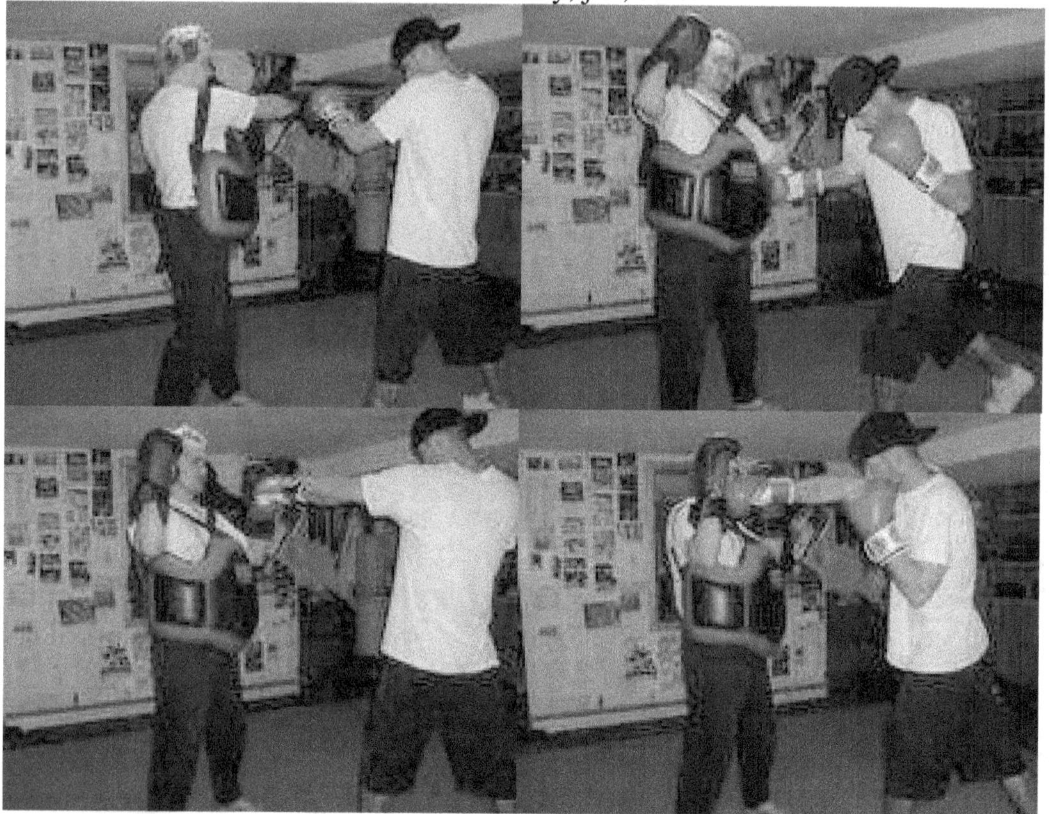

If you are throwing a reverse roundhouse kick to the thigh, try and have it slightly angled downward and hit the thigh with your shin. It's alright to hit with your instep, but you get a much harder hit using the shin. If you are doing point contact, you can use a shin or instep, it doesn't matter because that's just for points, but for a full contact competition, you are better off using the shin. 4 or 5 roundhouses to a thigh using a shin, will give about anyone a dead leg.

For set up on which way your roundhouse should go. If you are in a right stance as shown below, if the instructor throws a jab, you would parry with your left hand, then execute your reverse roundhouse. When you parry the strike, your opponent's back is more towards you.

If your coach throws a cross, you would parry the cross with your right hand and do a roundhouse to the inside of the thigh. The roundhouse would be slightly angled upward and make it a quick snap kick.

Note: in competition, all roundhouse kicks to the thigh should be at least 2" above the knee.

Interval uppercuts: stand square to the coach, uppercuts are done fairly quickly hitting the left glove to your coach's left mitt and the right hand to the coach's right mitt.

Straight punch intervals: throw left, right, left, right usually in 30-second intervals

Chapter 5
Stripe Test Level 3

Aaron Morris

Level 3

Level 3 Medicine Ball Routine
20 – sit-ups (pg. 30)
10 – sit-ups left elbow to right knee (pg. 30)
10 – sit-ups right elbow to left knee (pg. 30)
10 – sit-ups – chest to knee (pg 35)
10 – sit-ups – straight arm (pg. 36)
10 – sit-ups (pullover sit-ups) (pg. 72)
10 - sit-ups – V-ups (pg. 72)
10 – sit twist (pg. 72)
10 – sit and twist in crunch position (73)
Note: on the sit and twist, you start with one set of regular position, then go into the crunch position. Work your way up to 3 sets of 20. then finish the rest of the routine.
10 – superman (pg. 73)
10 – sitting overhead circles (pg. 74)
10 - seated overhead toe touch (pg. 74)
10 -- V-seated toe touch (pg. 75)
10 – V-seated giant circles (pg. 75)
30 – stabilization push-ups (alternating 2 feet and 1 foot) (pg. 76)
10 – Hip rotation (pg. 77)
10 – straight arm sit-up (pg. 36)
10 – cross leg sit-up (set of ten on both legs) (pg. 77)
10 – pelvic thrust (pg. 78)
10 – hip crunch (pg. 78)
10 – backward sit-up (pg. 78)
10 – supine knee to elbow (pg. 79)
10 – alternating toe touch (pg. 79)
10 – alternating toe touch with straight leg (pg. 79)
10 – seated single leg over and back (pg. 80)
10 – seated double leg over and back (pg. 80)
10 – seated hip adduction (pg. 81)
10 – inside leg left (pg. 81)
10 – side – lying hip abduction (pg. 82)
2 sets of 30 seconds – Plank (pg. 82)
2 sets of 30 seconds – Side Plank (pg. 82)

<u>Level 3 Coaches Mitts</u>

Round 1 Level 3

10 jab, cross, jab (pg. 37)
10 jab, cross, hook (pg. 38)
10 jab, cross, hook, reverse hook (pg. 39)
10 jab, cross, upper cut, reverse upper cut, jab cross (pg. 40)
10 jab, cross, leading hand hook to the body, leading hand hook to the head (pg. 62)
<u>Round 2 level 3</u>

Go through the 5 combos and add the defense against a hook. Throwing leading hand hook and reverse hooks at random to the body and head. When the hook goes to the body, the student uses an elbow block, when the hook goes to the head, the student will duck straight down, come up and execute jab, cross combination (pg. 83,84)

Note: the coach will go back and forth between the leading hand hook and reverse hook (so your coach will start you off with the first combo jab, cross, jab do maybe a couple of sets, and then throw in a hook to the body or head at random. Do 5 to 10 sets, then move to your next combo the jab, cross, hook, and then the coach slips in a hook to the body or hook to the head at random)

Note: on the combinations jab, cross hook, and jab, cross, hook, reverse hook, a lot of times I have the student put those hooks to the body. But when I'm running this block and counter exercise, were the counter hook is at the body, I usually have the student run the hook in the combo to the head.

<u>Round 3 Level 3</u>

In sets of 5 to 10 go back through the top 5 combinations, then mix in hooks to the body and head with the student using an elbow block for midsection defense and the back fist block at the head and counter with a hook to the body: If you block with the leading hand, you counter with a reverse hook, if you block with the reverse hand, then counter with a leading hand hook. Only counter to strikes to the head. (pg. 85)

Level 3 Medicine Ball

Sit-ups (pullover sit-ups)

Sit-ups – V-ups

Sit and Twist

Sit and Twist in a Crunch Position:

Note: you come down to about a 45% angle. Go side to side with the ball close to you. But to get a better stretch, when you go to the side reach out with the ball.

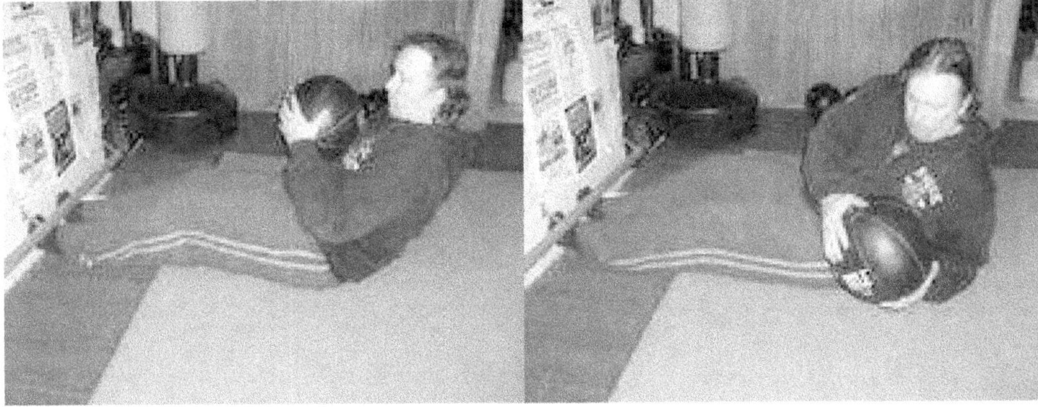

Superman: Arch your back and raise your feet at the same time, then down

Sitting Circles: With the ball over your head, move the ball in a circle

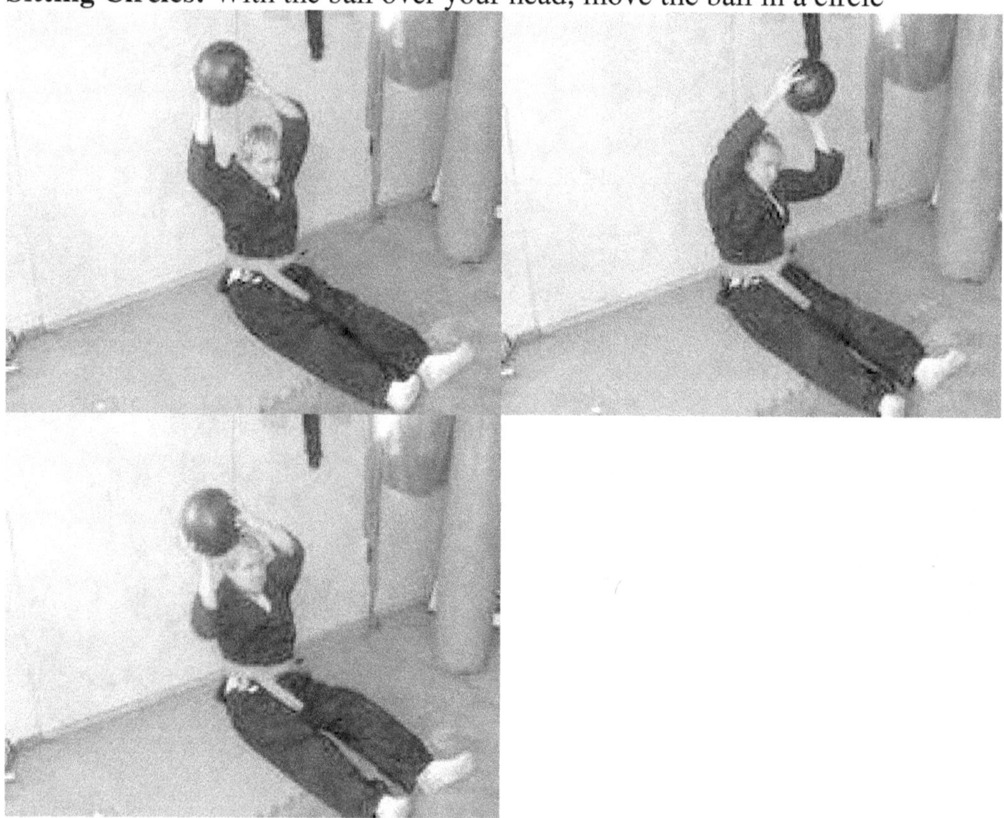

Seated Overhead Toe Touch: start at the back of the neck and touch your toes with the ball

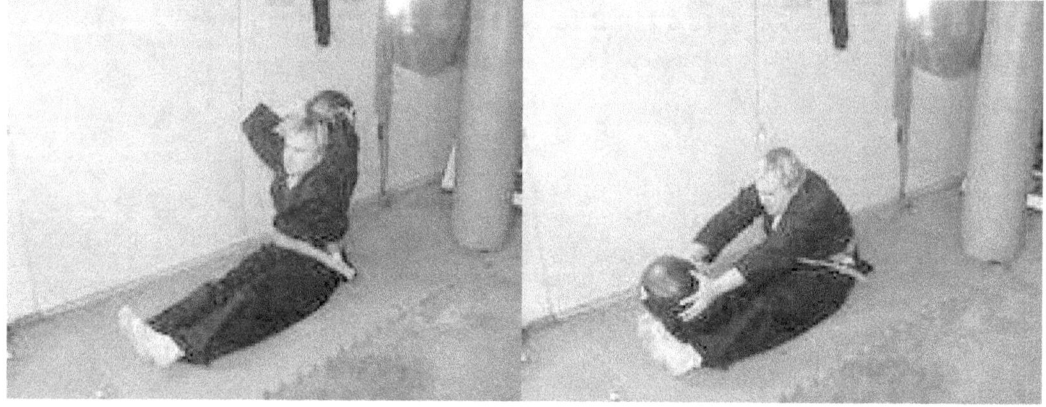

V Seated Toe Touch – start at the back of the neck, then touch your left toe, then back to the back of the neck, then touch your right toe)

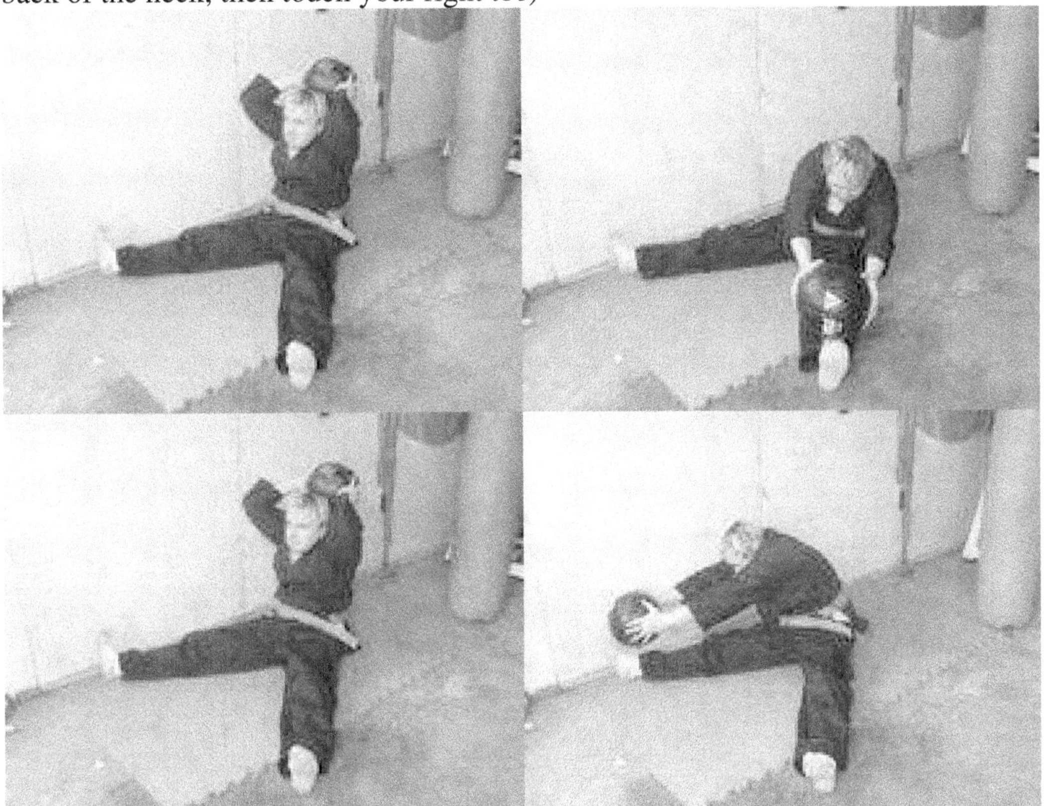

V-Seated Giant Circles – start with the ball over head then go to your right toe, on over to your left, turn your body so when you return to the ball over head, your side of your body is pulling you up, go counter clock wise 5 times then clock wise 5 times.

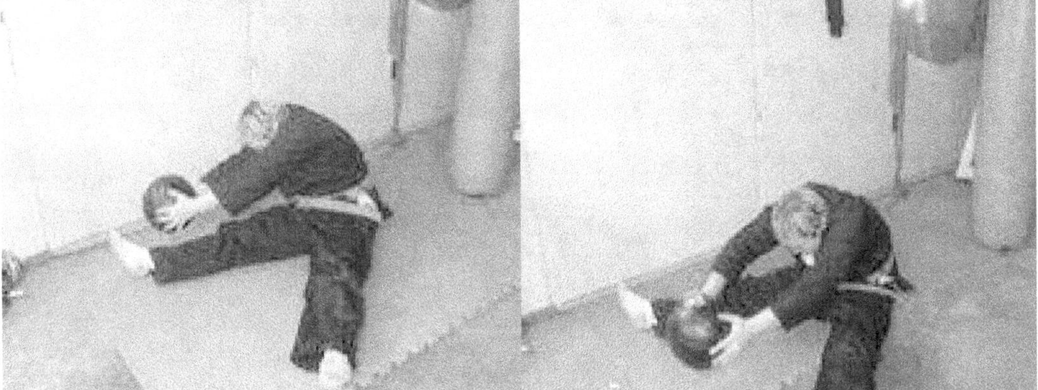

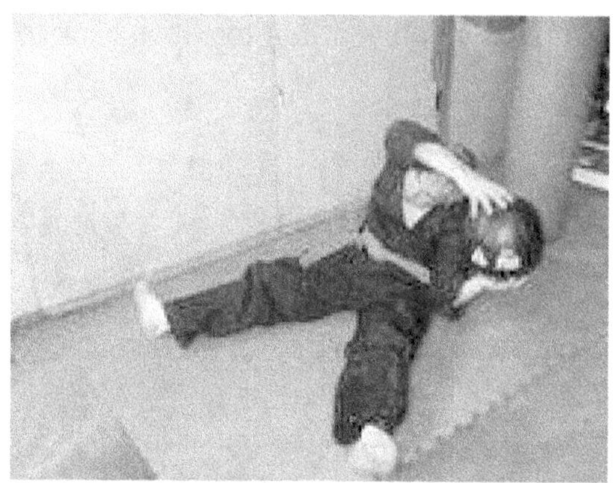

Stabilization Push-Ups: (alternating 2 feet and 1 foot)
2 feet on the ball

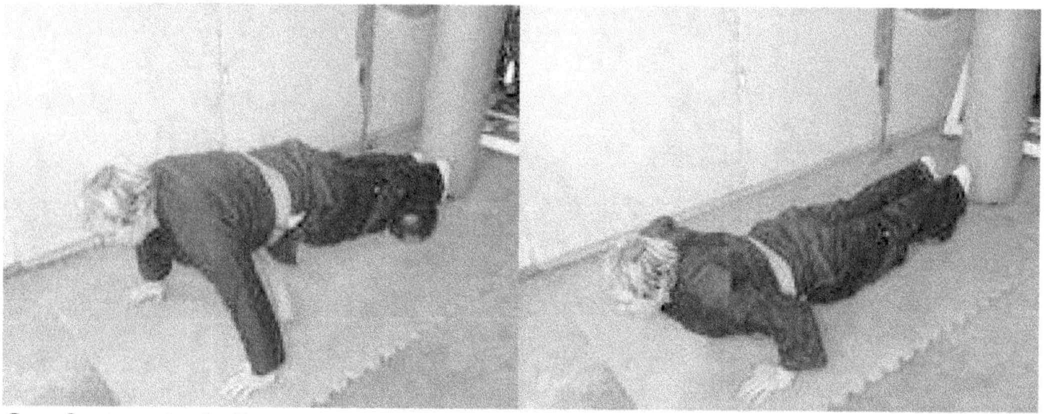

One foot on the ball

Hip Rotation: (may do this sitting at a 45% angle or lying down) *the medicine ball is between your knees and you rotate from side to side.*

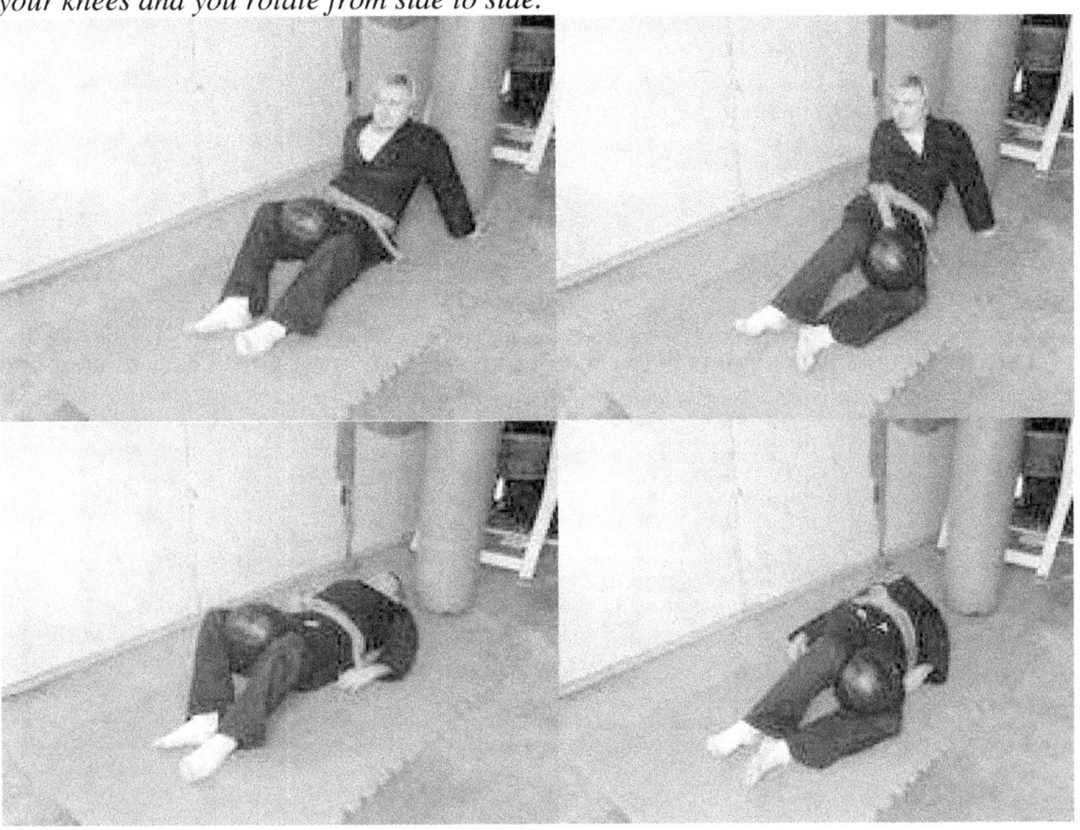

Cross Leg sit-up: (set of ten on both legs)

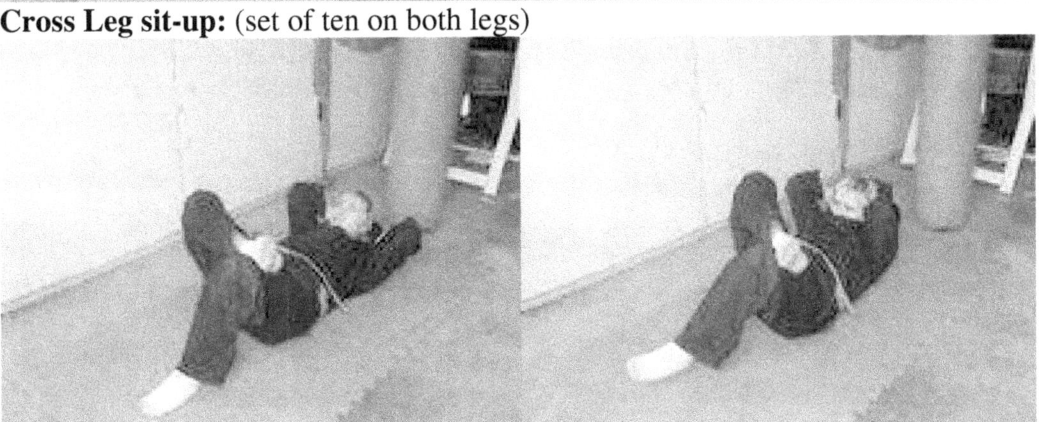

Pelvic Thrust: The m*edicine ball is between the legs and you bridge your hips up*

Hip Crunch: The medicine ball is between your knees. You bring your knees to your chest then back down to were your feet barely touch the floor, then back up.

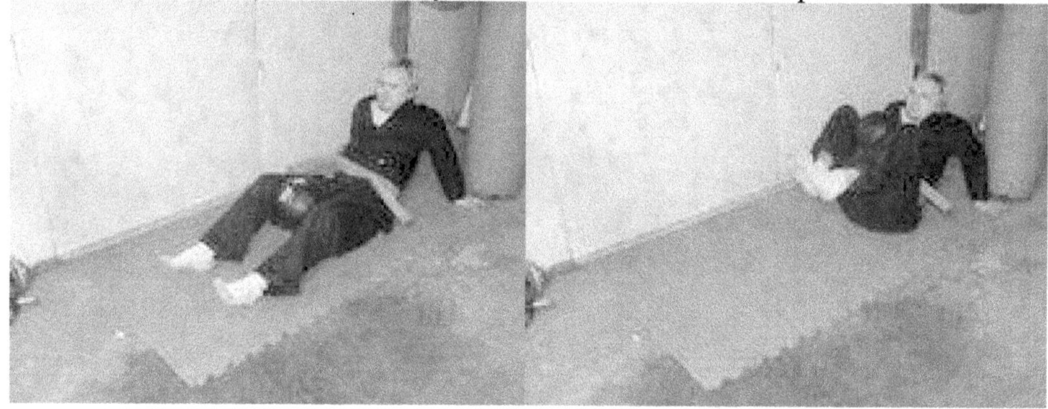

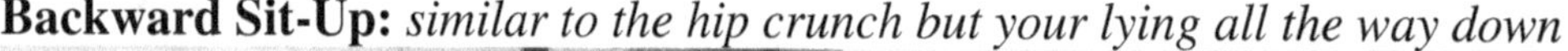

Backward Sit-Up: *similar to the hip crunch but your lying all the way down*

Supine knee to Elbow: *Lie on your back, bring your knee up and at the same time rotate your trunk and touch your elbow to your opposite knee)*

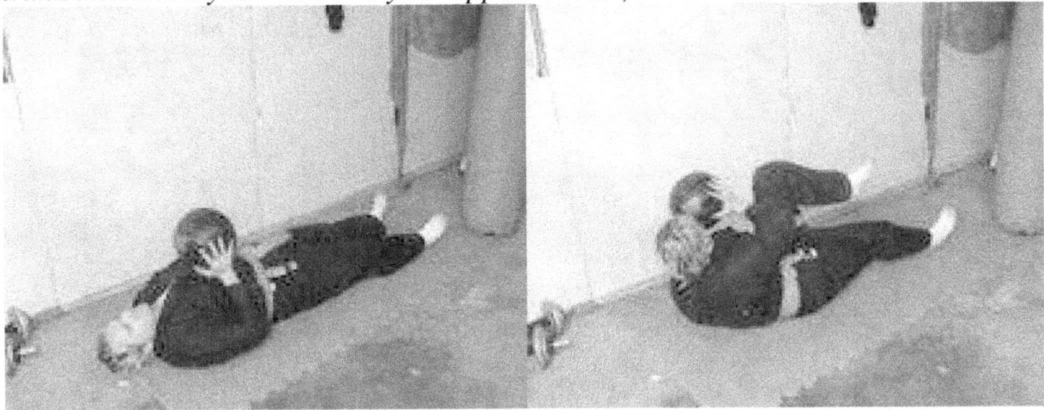

Alternating Toe Touch

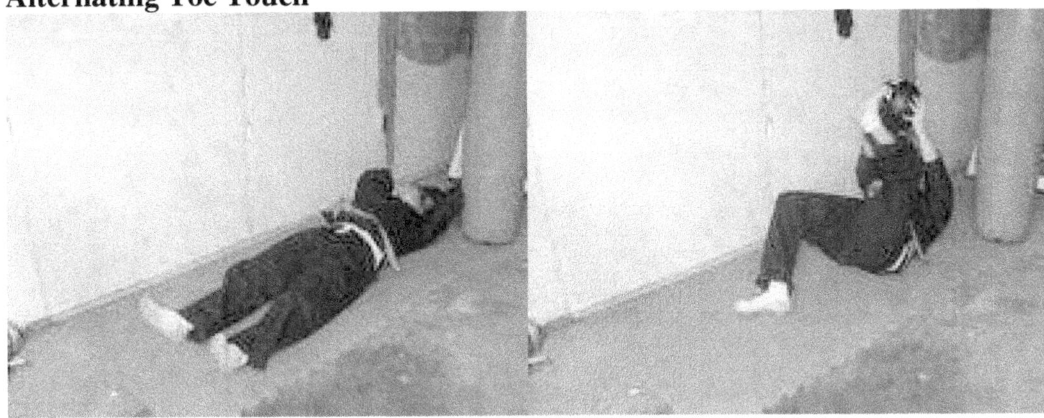

Alternating Toe Touch with Straight Leg

Seated Single Leg Over and Back: *start with both legs on one side of the ball, then move one foot over the ball to the other side then move the other and go back and forth one at a time.*

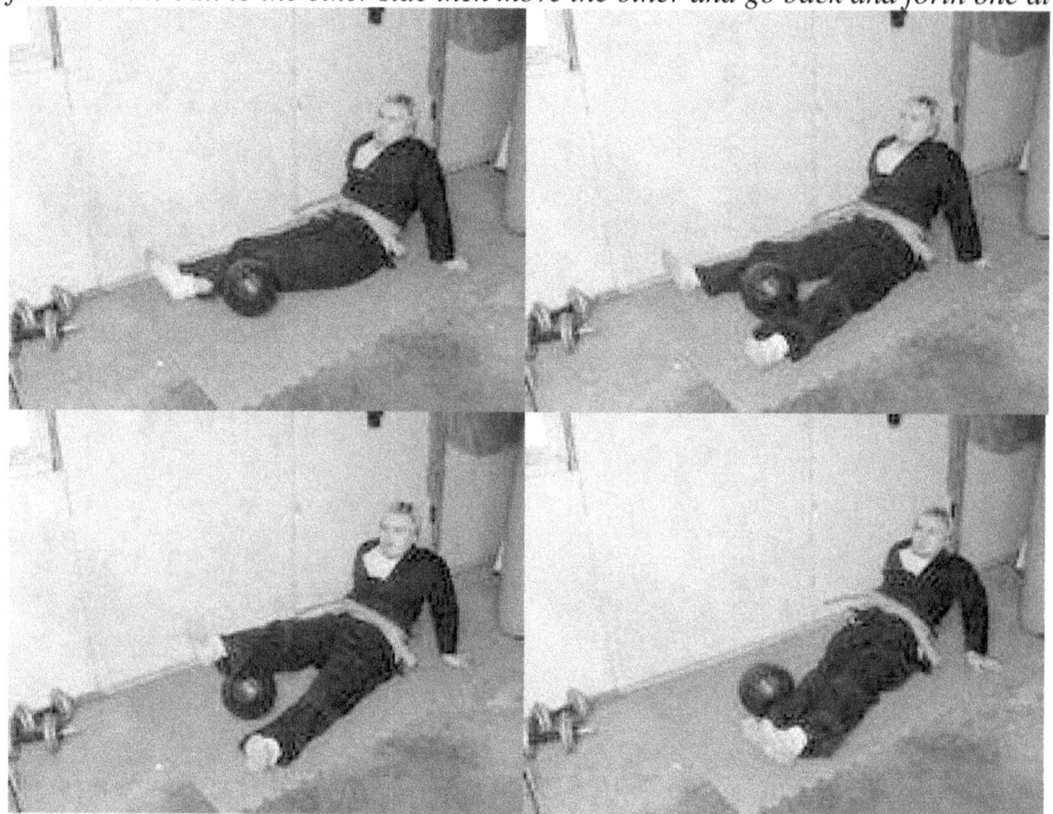

Seated Double Leg Over and Back: *start with both feet on one side of the ball and move them both at the same time over the ball barely touching the floor on each side of the ball and move back and forth.*

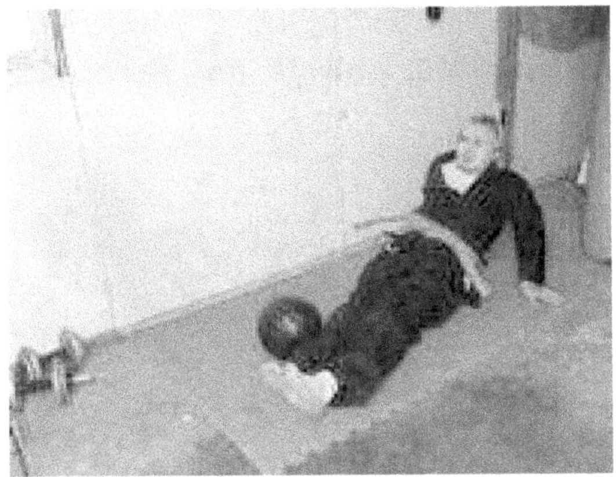

Seated Hip Adduction: *the ball will be on your thigh and you will lift your foot off the ground 10 to 12 inches straight up and down.*

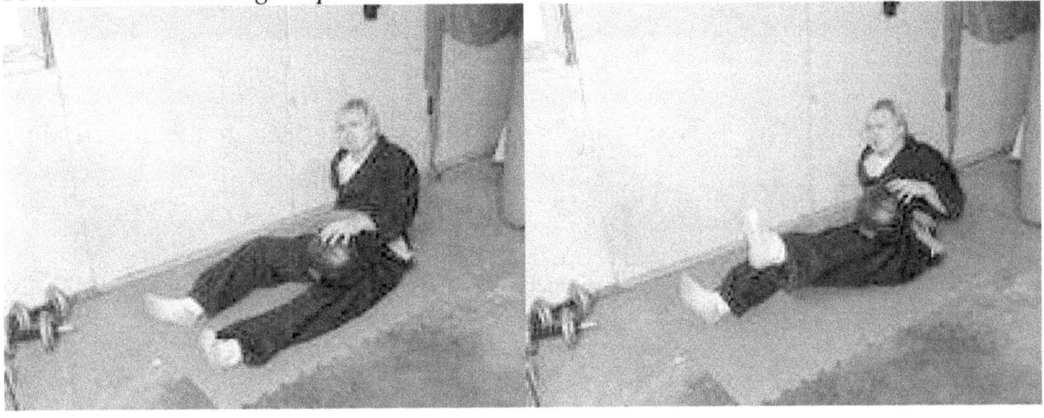

Inside Leg Left: *lie on your side and the ball will be on the inside of your thigh and you lift your leg 8 to 10 inches off the ground.*

Side – Lying Hip Abduction: *lie on your side, the ball will be about the area were your knee is and then raise your leg.*

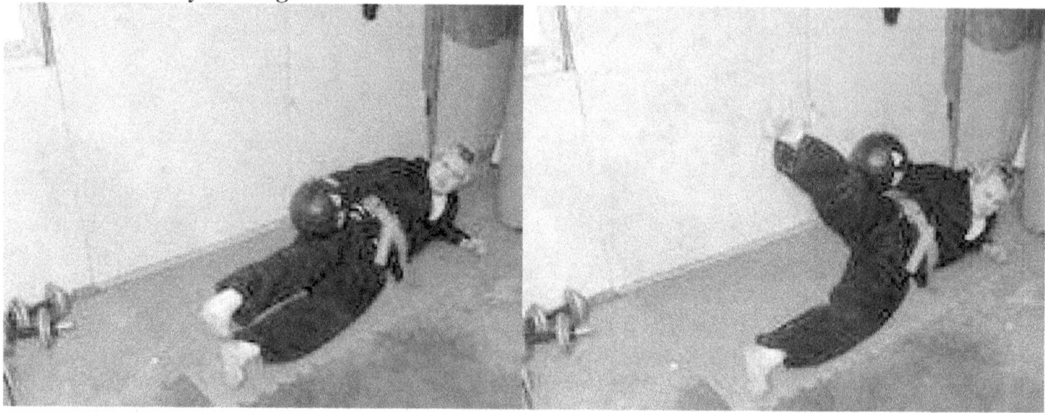

Plank

Note: you are up on your elbows. Keep your body straight and tighten up the muscles in your body

Side Plank:

Note: when doing this try and keep your body straight.

Level 3 Coaches Mitts

Elbow Block: this is a quick down and up motion) when a hook goes to the body, move your elbow down quickly to block the punch from hitting your side. Move your elbow down quickly and back up quickly.

Ducking under the hook: Note: don't bend forward on this. Come straight down. The student should keep his eyes on the coach at all times.

Duck under, 1, 2 – when the coach throws a hook, you duck under, then stand up and counter with a jab, cross combo.

Erick Rippe (student green belt January 2009)

Back fist Block

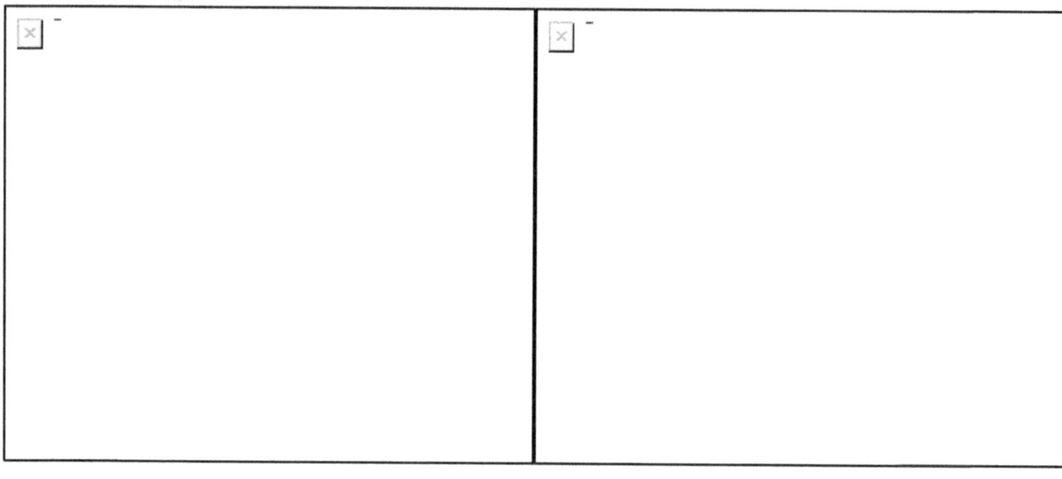

Back fist block with a counter hook to the body
(this is a defense against a lead hand hook to the head. On a back fist block, what you are doing is just covering up the side of your head with your fist. And the punch or kick lands on the back side of your hand rather than hitting you in the head) If you are blocking with the right hand, when you do that, you are setting up the counter strike with the left hand. The same thing goes if you are blocking with the left hand, you are looking for your target to be able to counter-strike with your right hand.

Chapter 6
Stripe Test Level 4

Rey Zuniga

Level 4 Medicine Ball Routine

Routine I
Run 1 mile

20 push-ups
20 sit-ups (pg. 30)
20 kick-outs (pg. 30)
10 Figure-8 (pg. 31)
10 circles (pg. 31)
10 side leg lifts (pg. 31)

Stretch

3X10 basketball pass (pg. 91)
3X10 overhead pass (pg. 91)
3X10 swing pass (pg. 92)
3X10 underhand pass (pg. 93)
3X10 back-to-back handoff (pg. 93)
3X10 basketball pass with one person standing and the other sitting on the ground *(to intensify that, do a sit up then pass) (pg. 94)*
3X10 back-to-back pass (standing about 3 feet apart) (pg. 95)
3X10 one-handed step-up reverse pass (pg. 96) *also called a shot put pass*
3X10 squat jump pass (pg. 97)

Note: you will do one set of each exercise then go back through and do your second set of each exercise, then go back through each medicine ball exercise and do your third set.

75 sit-ups

Routine II

Jump rope for 1 X 2 minutes
25 jumping jacks

Light stretch

2X2 minutes jump rope

20 push-ups
20 sit-ups (pg. 30)
20 kick-outs (pg. 30)
10 Figure-8 (pg. 31)
10 circles (pg. 31)
10 side leg lifts (pg. 31)

10 basketball pass (pg. 91)
10 overhead pass (pg. 91)
10 swing pass (pg. 92)
10 underhand pass (pg. 93)
10 back-to-back hand off (pg. 93)
10 basketball pass with one person standing and the other sitting on the ground *(to intensify that, do a sit up then pass) (pg. 94)*
10 back-to-back pass (standing about 3 feet apart) (pg. 95)
10 one-handed step-up reverse pass (pg. 96)
10 squat jump pass (pg. 97)

Light stretch

3X20 basketball pass (pg. 91)
3X20 overhead pass (pg. 91)
3X20 swing pass (pg. 92)
3X10 squat jump pass (pg. 97)

Level 4 Coaches Mitts

Round 1 level 4

10 jab, cross, jab (pg. 37)
10 jab, cross, hook (pg. 38)
10 jab, cross, hook, reverse hook (pg. 39)
10 jab, cross, duck, jab, cross (pg. 39)
10 jab, cross, uppercut, reverse uppercut, jab cross (pg. 40)
10 jab, cross, leading hand hook to the body, leading hand hook to the head (pg. 62)

Round 2 level 4

In round 2, you'll be going back through the combinations, but you'll also be using defense against the hook. Defense against the hook to the body will be an elbow block, and the hook to the head will be a back fist block, followed by an uppercut with the opposite hand.

► Coach throws a leading hand hook, the student does a reverse backhand block followed by a leading hand uppercut. (pg. 101)

► Coach throws a reverse hook, the student does a leading backhand block followed by a reverse uppercut. (pg. 101)

Round 3 Level 4

Working the double jab
The primary focus of this routine is working the jab. It's very important to know how to work the jab. This will help with controlling the pace of a bout. This will need to be done with speed and good snap. The number 1 is for a jab and the number 2 represents the cross. The combinations will be done in sets of 10.

1,1,2 (pg. 98) jab, jab, cross
1,2,1,2 or jab, cross, jab, cross
1,2, hook to the body (pg. 38) or jab, cross, hook
1,1,2 (pg. 98)
1,2, hook to the body lead hand, hook to the head lead hand (pg. 62)
1,2,1 walk-through combination (100)
1,1,2 (pg. 98)

Circuit training notes:
When running your circuit, there are a few different ways you can do it and it may depend on how many students you are working at a time. If I'm just working one fighter, I might go straight through one of the level workouts, doing 3 or 4 rounds on the mitts, and then from there, we would go to the bags. We have a speed bag, double-end bag, and heavy bag, we would change off each round go to a different bag, and do at least 2 sets on each bag, getting in 6 to 9 rounds on the bags and 3 or 4 rounds on the mitts. If you are working more than one fighter, then you run in a circuit, having different stations. One station will be the coach's mitts, then a speed bag, a heavy bag, and a double-end ball. But you can also add stations like a jump rope station, sit-up, stair climber or treadmill station, or even a push-up station. After each round, change to a different station. Doing that I try and get in 6 or 8 rounds and at least 2 rounds will be on the coaches mitts.

Notes on rounds: every round, usually takes 3 minutes. With as much coaching as I do, that's usually average for getting through each section. For a new person, the first time running the combinations may take a bit longer. But, I always do 3-minute rounds, with a 30-second break in between each round. For kids that are more advanced fighters, that round and break time frame works well. If you are just starting out a class with a bunch of new fighters, you may want to start out with 2-minute rounds with a 1-minute break, so you can spend a little time explaining the combinations and how to throw them properly. But, passing the level 1 boxing skill, you should be able to do 6 X 3 minute rounds with 30 second breaks and 2 of those rounds will be on the coach's mitts.

Basket Ball Pass: ball starts at your chest and you push out even with both hands

Overhead pass

Twist Pass:

Under Hand Pass

Back to Back Hand Off

Basket Ball Pass with one person standing and the other sitting on the ground *(to intensify that, do a sit-up up then pass. You can do a sit-up pass with the ball on your chest or you can have the ball overhead.)*

sit-up pass with the ball on your chest

sit-up pass with the ball overhead

Back-to-Back Pass: you stand back to back about 3 feet apart and go clockwise 5 to 10 times, then pass the medicine back counterclockwise 5 to 10 times.

One Handed Step-Up Reverse Pass (Shot Put Throw)

Squat Jump Pass: squat down and then jump as high as you can and do a chest pass as high up in the air as you can.

<u>Level 4 Coaches Mitts</u>

<u>1,1,2 (jab, jab, cross)</u>

1,2,1 (jab, cross, jab, cross)

Walk Threw Combination – Jab, step up and execute a cross, step down and execute a jab

Back Fist Block and Counter with a Uppercut

The coach does a lead hand hook. The student does a back fist block with his right hand and counters with a uppercut with his left.

The coach throws a reverse hook to the head, the student does a back fist block with the lead hand and counters with a reverse uppercut.

Chapter 7
Heavy Bag Routines

Heavy Bag Work-Out for Boxers
Routine #1

Warm-up

2-minute jump rope
25 jump jacks
stretch
2 X 2 Jump rope
30 push-ups
75 sit-ups (pg. 30)
20 kick outs (pg. 30)
10 figure eights (pg. 31)
10 circles (pg. 31)
10 side leg lifts (pg. 31)

Hitting the heavy bag

20 jab, cross, jab (pg. 105)
20 jab, cross, hook (pg. 105)
20 jab, cross, hook, reverse hook (pg. 106)

Light stretch

Jab, Cross, Jab

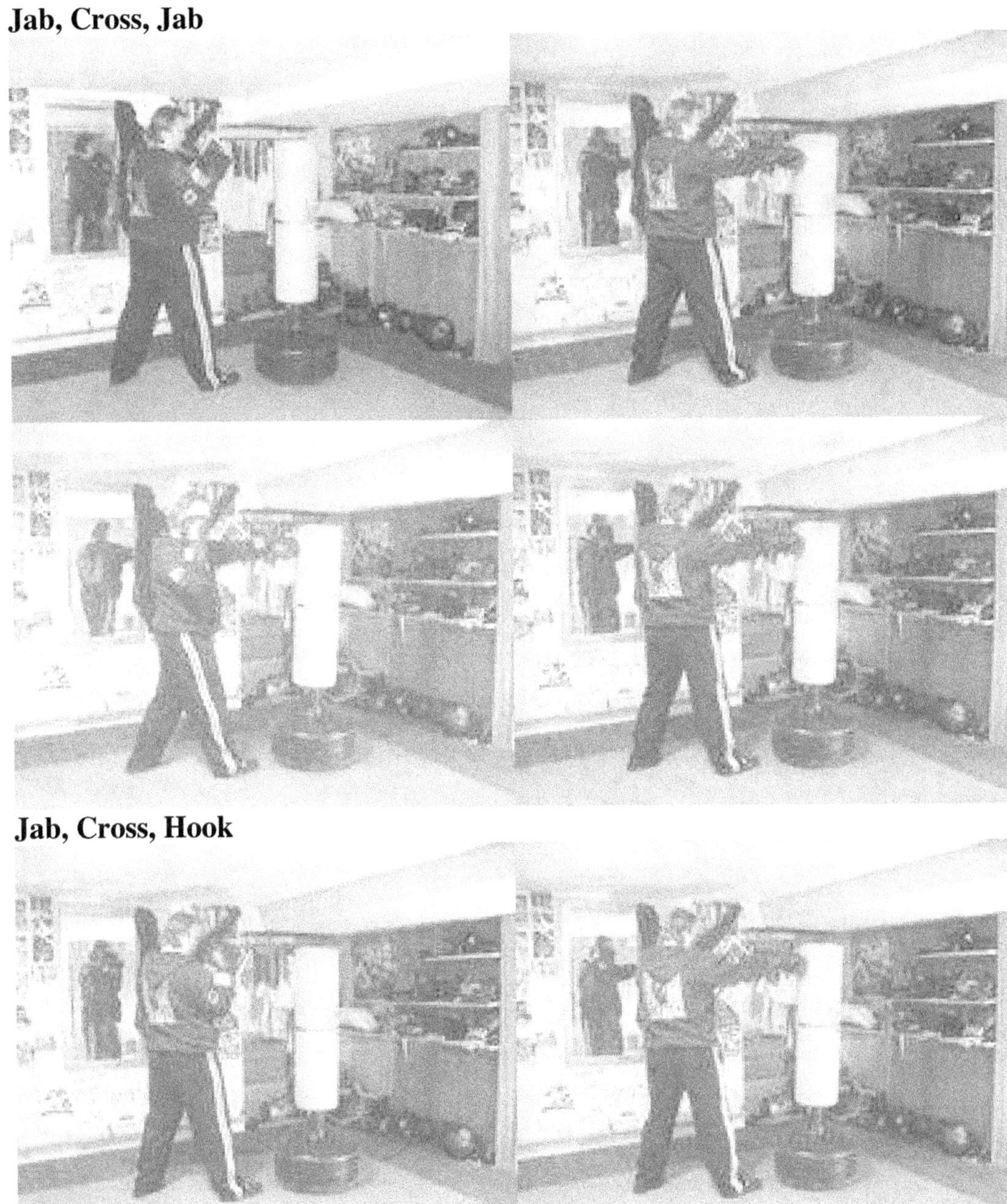

Jab, Cross, Hook

Jab, Cross, Hook, Reverse Hook

Heavy Bag Work-Out For Boxers
Routine #2

Warm-up

2-minute jump rope
25 jump jacks
stretch
2 X 2 Jump rope
30 push-ups
75 sit-ups
20 kick outs
10 figure eights
10 circles
10 side leg lifts

Hitting the heavy bag

10 jab
10 double jab
10 triple jab
10 quadruple jab (pg. 108) *Note: on each jab, try and bring the hand back to your cheek each to build tone on throwing a full jab*

10 cross
10 double cross
10 triple cross
10 quadruple cross (pg. 108) *Note: After each cross, bring your hand, back by your cheek and pivot your hips back. Full extensions each time will help develop speed and power)*

10 front to back (jab, cross) (pg. 109)
10 side to side (jab, cross)

20 jab, cross, jab (pg. 110)
20 jab, cross, hook (pg, 111)
20 jab, cross, hook, reverse hook (pg. 111)

Light stretch

Jab, Jab: *bring your fist back after each jab to the ready position. Your right hand stays by your cheek*

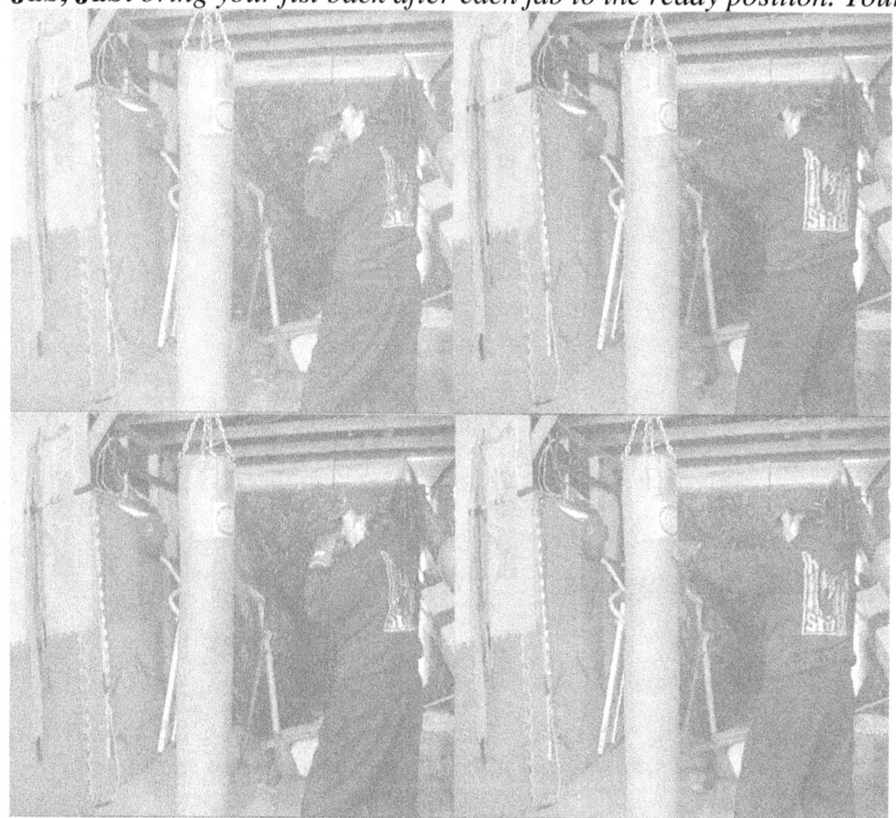

Cross, Cross: after each cross, you bring your right hand back to your cheek to ready stance then execute another one. When executing your cross your left hand stays by your cheek.

...le to Side and Front to Back: In a left stance, if the coach moves the bag to your right, you step ...ur right foot over, then your left foot and execute a jab cross, then the coach moves the bag to your ... and you move your left foot to your left then bring your right foot over and execute a jab, cross combo. ...his exercise, you are working on your combinations and working on proper stepping. ...ually do a set of 10 to 20. Then go into front-to-back, when the coach moves the bag backward, you ...vance, stepping with your lead foot, and when that lead foot lands on the ground you should be ...cuting a jab at the same time and follow up with a cross and bringing your right foot up about 6 to 8 ...hes so you are not over-extended. When moving back, you move your right foot back 6 to 8 inches and ...ng your left foot back. The coach will move the bag towards you and you execute a jab, cross combo. ...te: You step to the left, then do your combo, step to the right and do your combo, and repeat 10 times. ...p forward, then do your combo, step back and do your combo, and repeat 10 times.

Jab, Cross, Jab

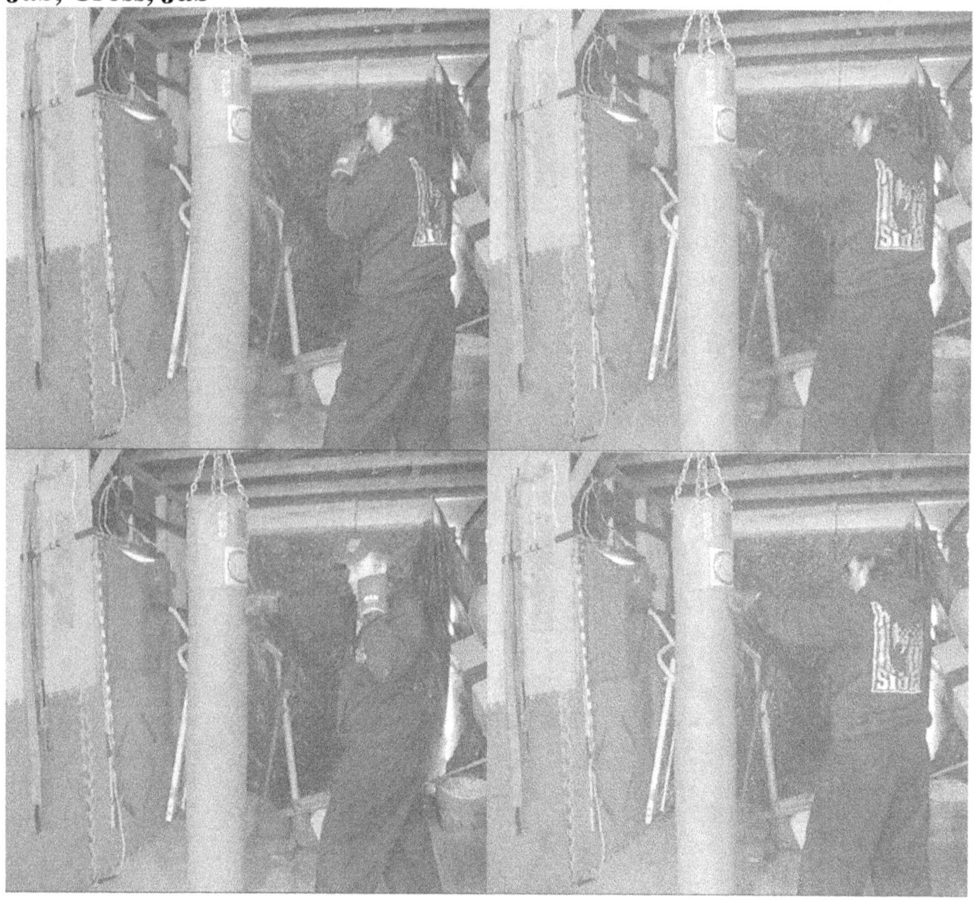

b, Cross, Hook

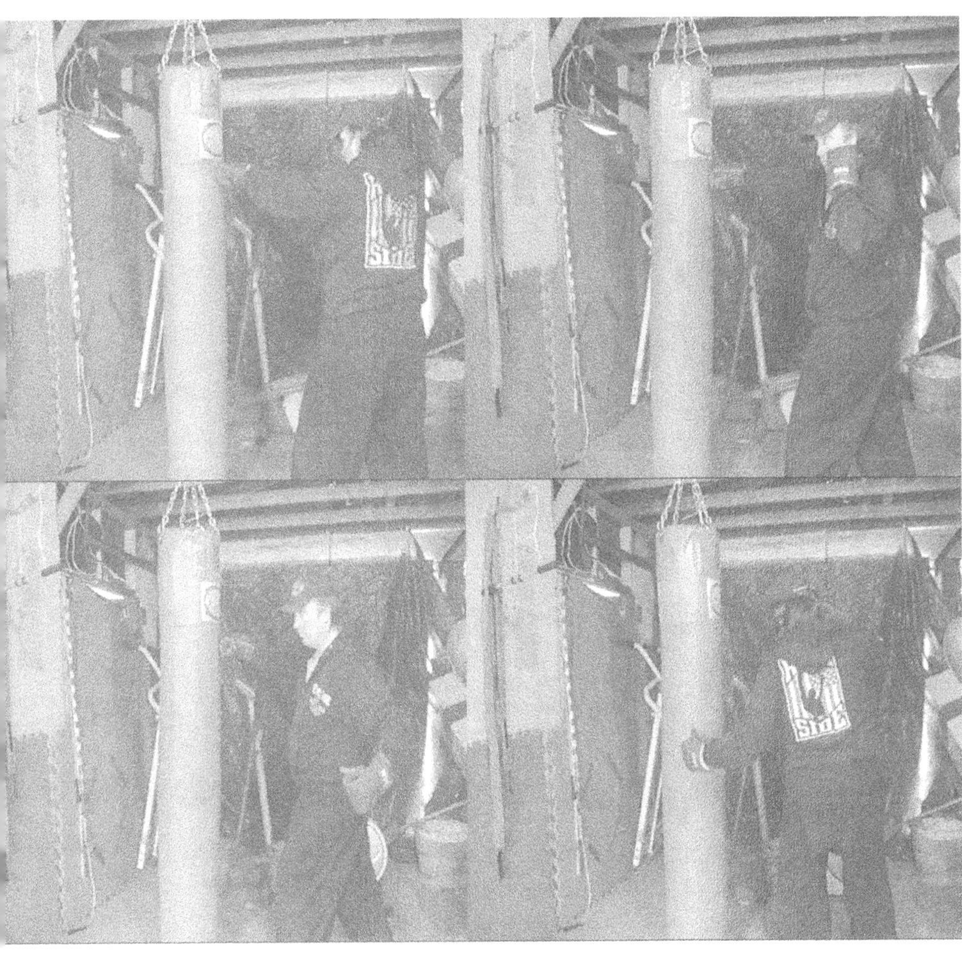

b, Cross, Hook, Reverse Hook

Heavy Bag Workout for KickBoxing
Routine #3

Warm-up
2 minutes jump rope
25 jump jacks

stretch

30 pushups
30 sit-ups
20 kick-outs
10 figure 8
10 circles
10 side leg lifts

Hitting the heavy bag

10 single jabs (pg. 108)
10 double jabs
10 triple jabs

10 single crosses (pg. 108)
10 double-crosses
10 triple crosses

20 jab, cross, jab
20 jab, cross, hook (midsection)
20 jab, cross, hook (midsection), reverse hook (midsection)

10 reverse front kick (pg. 114)
20 reverse front kick, step down, 1,2 step back 1,2 (pg. 114)
20 reverse front kick, step down 1,2 step back 1,2,1,2 (pg. 116)
10 reverse front kick (pg. 114)
20 side kicks to the midsection
20 double round-houses (round-house to the midsection, round-house head high)
10 reverse front kick, step down 1,2 step back 1,2, hook to the midsection, reverse hook to the midsection, hook to the head (pg. 118)

20 hook-kick, round-house combo (both head high)

Note: all 1,2 or jab, cross combos are to the head

Reverse Front Kick

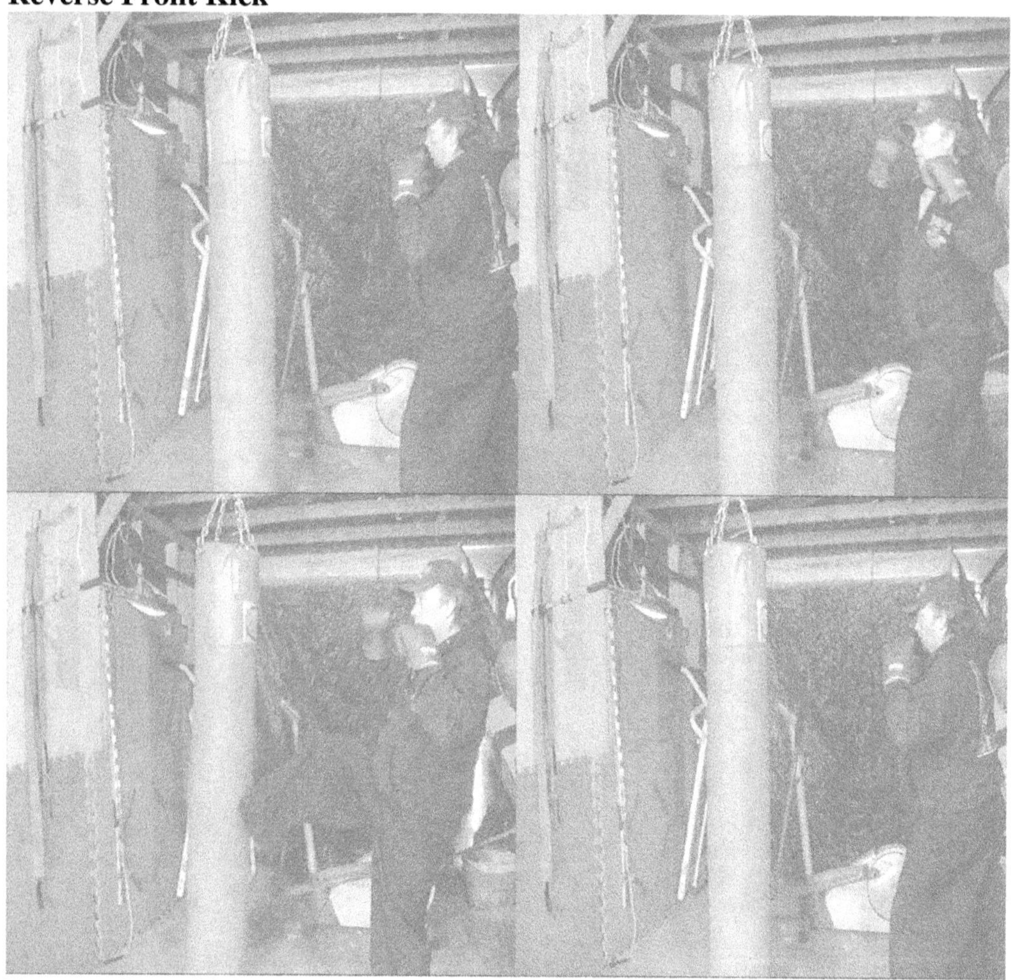

Reverse front kick, step down, 1,2 step back 1,2

Reverse front kick, step down 1,2 step back 1,2,1,2

Reverse front kick, step down 1,2 step back 1,2, hook to the midsection, reverse hook to the midsection, hook to the head

Reverse Front Kick

Jab   Cross

bring your right foot back
.and execute a Jab   Cross

Lead hook to the body

Reverse hook to the body

Lead hook to the head

Heavy Bag Workout For KickBoxing
Routine #4

Warm-up
2 minutes jump rope
25 jump jacks

stretch

30 pushups
20 sit-ups
20 kick-outs
10 figure 8
10 circles
10 side leg lifts

Hitting the heavy bag

10 single jabs
10 double jabs
10 triple jabs

10 single cross
10 double cross
10 triple cross

20 jab, cross, jab
20 jab, cross, hook (midsection)
20 jab, cross, hook (midsection), reverse hook (midsection)

20 set-ups

10 reverse front kick
20 reverse front kick, step down, 1,2 step back 1,2
20 reverse front kick, step down 1,2 step back 1,2,1,2

20 set-ups

10 reverse front kick
20 side kicks
20 double roundhouses
10 reverse front kick, step down 1,2 step back 1,2, hook to the midsection, reverse hook to the midsection, hook to the head

20 set-ups

20 hook-kick, roundhouse combo
3 sets of 10 triple roundhouse kicks

Note: all 1,2 or jab, cross combos are to the head
Note: as you get better in shape you might increase the set-ups to 50, and then if you need to increase even more, I'd add holding a medicine ball.
Note: 350 kicks and 800 punches
Note: on the first set of kicks I usually wear ankle weights. I don't recommend them, but I do what I can to add speed and power to my kicks.

Chapter 8
Speed Drills

From left to right: Erick Rippe, Bryce Adamson, and Aaron Morris

Speed drill #1

10 jabs
9 jabs
8 jabs
7 jabs
6 jabs
5 jabs
4 jabs
3 jabs
2 jabs
1 jab

Do the same with the Cross

Do the same with a roundhouse kick, left leg then switch and do the right leg

Speed drill #2

10 front kicks to the heavy bag or kicking pad
switch and do 10 front kicks with the other leg, bringing the foot back to the ground on every
kick.

Speed drill #3

Reverse roundhouse drill on a kicking bag or heavy bag
Single reverse roundhouse, double reverse roundhouse, triple reverse roundhouse bringing the
leg back and touching the ground before executing another roundhouse
Switch and do the other leg. Do a set of 10.

Speed Drill #4

Stand in a horse stance: both feet are pointed forward and your knees are bent. When one hand is out on a punch the other retracts to your side to get a full extension.

Do 10 sets of single punches
10 sets of double punches
10 sets of triple punches
10 sets of 4
10 sets of 5
10 sets of 6
10 sets of 7
10 sets of 8
10 sets of 9
10 sets of 10

Speed Drill #5

Progressive combos: In a Progressive combination routine you do a set of 10 on a combination, then add an extra strike or block after each set. You may start off with a block, strike combination, but after the 5th set, it may be a 6 block/strike combination. On this progressive combo, you start off with the coach stepping in and executing a lunge punch, the student does a leading hand palm block or parry. You do a set of 10, parry then counter with a vertical punch. After you are done with that set of ten, then add another strike. Your next strike would be the elbow strike. So you would run the combo, parry, vertical punch, elbow strike

Routine Outline:

Set of 10 -- Coacher steps forward and delivers a Lunge punch, the students Parries and executes a Vertical punch to the midsection

Set of 10 -- Coacher steps forward and delivers a Lunge punch, the student Parries and executes a Vertical punch to the midsection, leading elbow strike to the head

Set of 10 -- Coacher steps forward and delivers a Lunge punch, the student Parries and executes a Vertical punch to the midsection, leading elbow strike to the head, a back-fist strike with the leading hand

Set of 10 -- Coacher steps forward and delivers a Lunge punch, the student Parries and executes a Vertical punch to the midsection, a leading elbow strike to the head, a back-fist strike with the leading hand, vertical punch to the stomach

Set of 10 -- Coach steps forward and delivers a Lunge punch, the students Parries and executes a Vertical punch to the midsection, a leading elbow strike to the head, a back-fist strike with the leading hand, a vertical punch to the stomach, a leading hand uppercut

the basic theory on that combo is if you are shifting your weight one way, you hit twice, shift the other way you hit twice again and it ends up being a pretty fluent combo. And it looks cool when hitting the heavy bag with it.

Set of 10 -- Parry block, counter with a vertical punch to the midsection

Set of 10 -- Parry block, counter with a vertical punch to the midsection, elbow strike

Set of 10 -- Parry block, counter with a vertical punch to the midsection, elbow strike, back fist strike

Set of 10 -- Parry block, counter with a vertical punch to the midsection, elbow strike, back fist strike, vertical punch

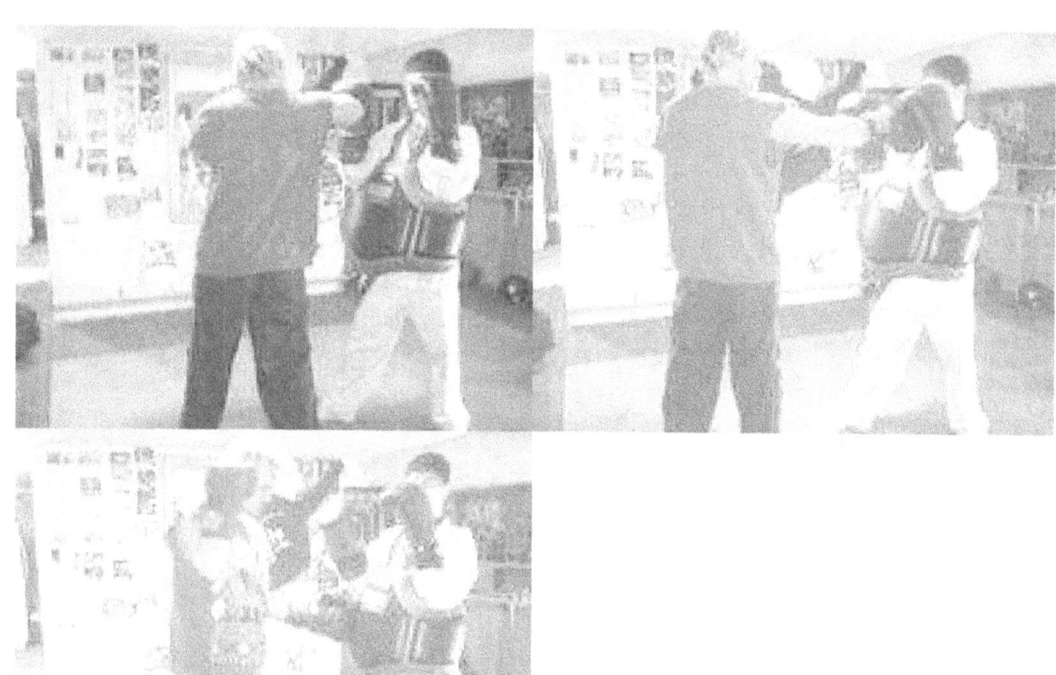

Set of 10 -- Parry block, counter with a vertical punch to the midsection, elbow strike, back fist strike, vertical punch, uppercut

Note: In a progressive combination you can modify it to fit your own personal style or need. Another progressive combo example would be something along the line of the coach would step forward and do a lunge punch, the students' ending combination total would be a parry, reverse roundhouse to the thigh, lead leg roundhouse to the inside of the thigh, jab, cross, uppercut. For a progressive combo, you just break it down into sections as shown for speed drill #5.

Speed Drill #6 (this routine will be shown in the heavy bag training section)

This one works best on the heavy bag but can be done on the kicking pad

10 single jabs
10 double jabs
10 triple jabs

10 single crosses
10 double-crosses
10 triple crosses

20 jab, cross, jab
20 jab, cross, hook (midsection)
20 jab, cross, hook (midsection), reverse hook (midsection)

10 reverse front kick
20 reverse front kick, step down, 1,2 step back 1,2
20 reverse front kick, step down 1,2 step back 1,2,1,2
10 reverse front kick
20 reverse front kick, step down 1,2 step back 1,2,1,2
20 side kicks
20 reverse front kick, step down 1,2 step back 1,2, hook to the midsection, reverse hook to the midsection, hook to the head

20 double roundhouse
20 hook-kick, round house combo

Note: all 1,2 or jab, cross combos are to the head

Speed Drill #7

The coach keeps a kicking pad on his thigh and does a cross
The student does a leading hand parry block followed by a roundhouse to the thigh. Do a set of
10 to the thigh, then a set of 10 to the midsection, then a set of 10 at head high, then the coach
switch legs and stance, then the student will parry the cross, do a half step back, and execute the
roundhouse to the thigh, midsection, and head, executing a set of 10 at each target area.

Parry, roundhouse to the thigh

Parry, roundhouse to the midsection

parry, roundhouse to the head

8.6

the coach switches stances to a left stance, but the student stays in his right stance. The coach throws a cross, the student parries with the left hand, does a half step back with his right foot, then executes a roundhouse to the left thigh of the coach. *Note: when your leg comes back on that half step, you are coming back a half step to ¾ back, but not quite back to a full step that would put you in a left stance.*

The coach throws a cross, the student parries with the left hand, does a half step back with his right foot, and then executes a roundhouse to the midsection of the coach.

The coach throws a cross, the student parries with the left hand, does a half step back with his right foot, and then executes a roundhouse to the head of the coach.

Speed Drill #8
1,2 reverse front kick, step down, 1,2 reverse front kick
reverse knee strike, step down, reverse knee strike
reverse roundhouse, step down, 1,2, reverse roundhouse, step down, 1, 2
These are all reverse kicks and you switch legs on each strike. Do a set of 10 on the kicking pad

Speed Drill #9
Change Ups:
Start in a left stance, execute a right reverse roundhouse, bring it back, and then execute another reverse roundhouse. After the second roundhouse instead of bringing it back, you step it down, so now you are in your right stance, then execute a reverse roundhouse, bring it back so you are in a right stance, then execute a second reverse roundhouse, and after the second roundhouse instead of bringing the roundhouse back, you drop it down so now you are in a left stance. *(note: I'd do this routine with your regular circuit hitting the other bags or other circuits, maybe in 2 or 3-minute spurts or in sets of 20.)*

From your second reverse roundhouse kick bring your left foot down beside your right foot, then step your right foot back into a left stance and set up for your reverse rounds house in your right stance

Speed Drill #10
Working the Back-Fist Strike:
Jab, spinning back fist
Jab, spinning back fist, spinning back fist
Jab, cross, jab, spinning back fist, spinning back fist
Reverse front kick to the midsection, jab followed by a step threw spinning back-fist. *Note: the jab is used as a fake to set you up for your spinning back fist so it's less likely to be telegraphed Note: the back fist drills are good to practice on coaches' mitts or on a heavy bag as shown below.*
Jab, Spinning Back Fist

Jab, Spinning Back Fist, Spinning Back Fist

Jab, cross, jab, spinning back fist, spinning back fist

Jab, cross, jab, spinning back fist, spinning back fist

Reverse front kick to the midsection, jab followed by a step threw spinning back-fist

Chapter 9
Team Drills

Team Drills #1

5 to 1

with this team drill, we'll use a heavy bag. One that sits on the ground works pretty well. You'll do a set of 5 roundhouses without putting your foot down, then you'll do two reverse roundhouses to the thigh area. The roundhouse off the leading leg needs to be to the midsection or head high, the reverse roundhouse is supposed to be to the thigh area and should be angled slightly downward. So you'll start off with 5 lead leg round houses, then two reverse round houses. Then as soon as one person finishes his combo, the next person will do that combination. I usually go clockwise in my rotation. After everyone does their set they do a set of 4 lead leg round houses, then 2 reverse round houses, then 3 lead leg round houses and two reverse round houses, then two lead leg round houses and 2 reverse round houses, then 1 lead leg round houses and 2 reverse round houses. Then switch stance and start all over. I usually start kids off with 3 sets on both stances. *(this speed drill works to develop speed coming off your lead leg and develop power coming off your reverse as well as help with developing balance. For the competition, most likely you won't do 5 round houses in a row, but a 2 and 3-step combo with a lead leg is common, but it has to be done quickly and you'll need good balance).*

On the lead leg round houses, you're kicking midsection to head high. You do your set of 5 without putting your leg down.

For the two reverse roundhouses, you want to throw your roundhouse at thigh level and bring it back after each roundhouse. This will help get your reverse kicks get off the ground and executed quicker. Anything coming from the reverse has to be pretty quick so it doesn't get telegraphed. Work on technique and balance. There shouldn't be much stepping around getting set for each set. The less amount of stepping or swaying around, the less likely you'll telegraph your kicks.

Speed Drill #2
Jab, cross, lead leg roundhouse, jab, cross. Set a timer at 3 minutes. When one person gets done with the combination, then the next person does the combination. Then the next and it keeps going around in a circle rotating who does the combination.

Rest for 30 seconds then go to the next combo for a 3-minute round
Jab, cross, lead leg roundhouse, jab, cross, reverse roundhouse. This adds the reverse roundhouse in the last technique.

Speed Drill #3
Work on footing
step, step, Jab, cross
this will work on your step work. You'll start off by going clockwise around the bag for a minute or two minutes, then go counterclockwise. Be in your regular fight stance for this drill. If you have your right leg forward, when going clockwise you would move your right foot to the right, then bring your left foot to the right, then execute a jab, cross combo. If you are moving counterclockwise you would move your left foot to the left, then bring your right foot over. This type of stepping is for pressure fighting and staying on the inside. Your focus is on the center of the bag or when sparring your focus is in the middle of the chest. When stepping to the side this way your feet don't cross.

Stepping to the right or clockwise: step the right foot to the right, then move the left foot over, then execute jab, cross

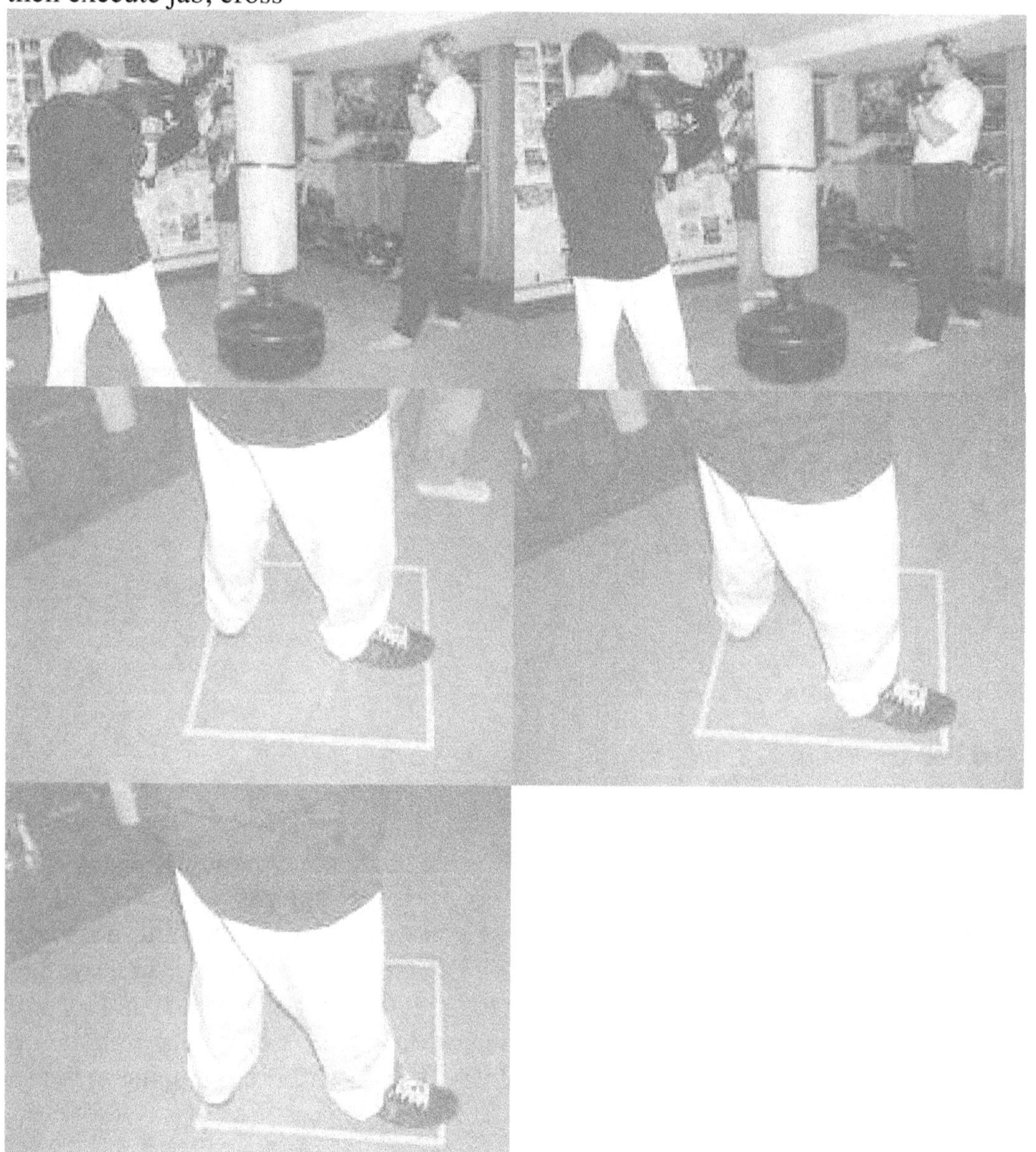

stepping to the left or counter-clockwise: step the left foot to the left, then bring the right foot over, then execute a jab, cross

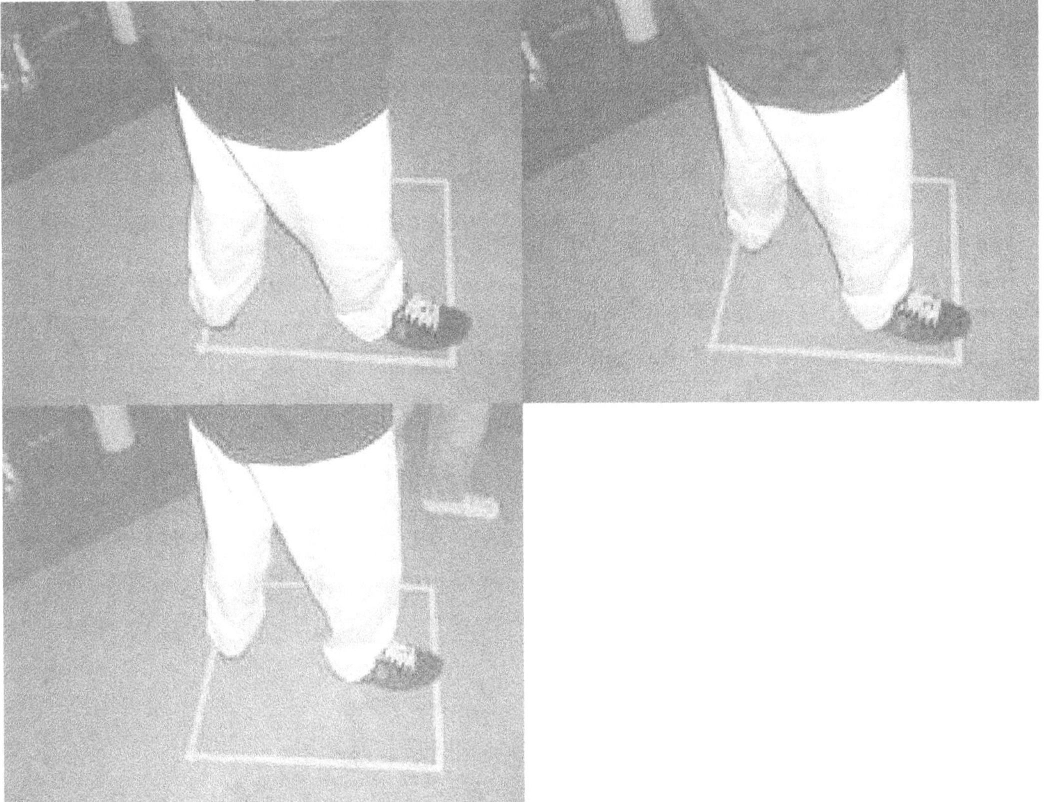

"6 day a week training program for Kick-boxers"

Monday, Wednesday, and Friday Routine

15 minutes on the runner
4 rounds 2 minutes long going back and forth between the speed bag and double-end ball

20 sit-ups
10 sit-ups -- chest to toe (pg.35)
10 sit ups -- chest to knee (pg35)
10 sit ups -- straight arm (pg. 36)
20 kick-outs (pg. 30)
10 Figure 8 (pg. 31)
10 circles (pg. 31)

2 sets of the 5 to 1 speed drill as shown on team drill #1 : (start off with 2 sets and work your way up to 5)

5 round houses (pick up the leg and do 5 round houses without putting your leg down)
2 reverse roundhouse (the reverse roundhouse should be thigh level and chop down, after each kick, bring back the leg to the original stance and kick again)
4 round houses
2 reverse round houses
3 double round houses
2 reverse round houses
2 lead leg round houses
2 reverse round houses
1 leading leg roundhouse
2 reverse round houses

Tuesday, Thursday, and Saturday
5X10 Squats
5 X 20 Leg extensions
5X20 Leg Curls
2X10 1 leg squat
2 X 20 Calve raises
On Tuesdays do medicine ball routine #2, on Thursdays do Medicine ball routine #3.

Note: when trying to develop quickness in the feet, sometimes I look at some of the hand techniques. My theory is, that if you want to equal out your feet and hand techniques, you should be able to develop similar routines. Like the 1 to 10 burnout routine that's in my first book. Where you do single punches, 10 sets of 1, then go 10 sets of 2, then 10 sets of 3, all the way up to 10 sets of 10, then you work your way back to 10 sets of 1. It's a good burnout routine, but not too many people make it through that routine the first few times. Usually, I just go up to 5 or 7 when I'm teaching, but it would depend on how in shape my students are. But, what I was trying to do with the kicks was the 5 to 1. Were you start off with a pick-up roundhouse from the leading leg, do 5 round houses before putting your leg down again, step back into your stance, then do a set of 4, then a set of 3, then a set of 2, then a set of 1. I was doing that as part of a circuit and doing a 3-minute round, doing 5 to 1 with one leg, then switching back and forth doing each leg. I started doing this because I was having a hard time getting one of my students to use his leading leg more. He was always doing a reverse kick and he was telegraphing his kick and with a point tournament coming up, 90% of your kicks have to come from a leading leg. but in full contact, you gotta develop your reverse kick. So I went and modified the 5 to 1 routine. To picking up your leg, doing the set of 5 round houses, then put your foot down, and do 2 reverse round houses. This is to help develop the reverse roundhouse to the thigh. So on the reverse roundhouse, you want that kick to chop down as in chopping down on a thigh. Gotta develop that natural type of kick, and with a roundhouse to the thigh, I usually try and hit with the shin. But if it goes to the body or head, I usually use the instep.

With the routines, I have set up for T, Th, and Sa with the weight lifting. I developed that to try to get my legs stronger and to rehab my knee. Hurt my knee a couple of years ago and it hasn't healed very well. I've babied it long enough, now it's time to push it and see what it does. A lot of times, doing some weight training will work out the kinks.

On the sit-ups, the primary goal for a professional is trying to get up to 300 sit-ups each day. That's a minimum. I like the setup I have with the routines, where you do 5 or 6 different sit-ups. You might do one set, each day with what I have written up, but then you could put that in segments throughout your routine. Get up to 20 sit-ups on each style of sit-up, then, go into segments throughout your routine and maybe get in 3 or 4 sets, to get ya over 300. But, when I get students complaining about that, I usually just tell them, Well Mike Tyson would do 2500 per day, so 300 really isn't all that much. but, building a strong core is a key to developing powerful kicks and punches.

Chapter 10
How to Wrap Your Hands

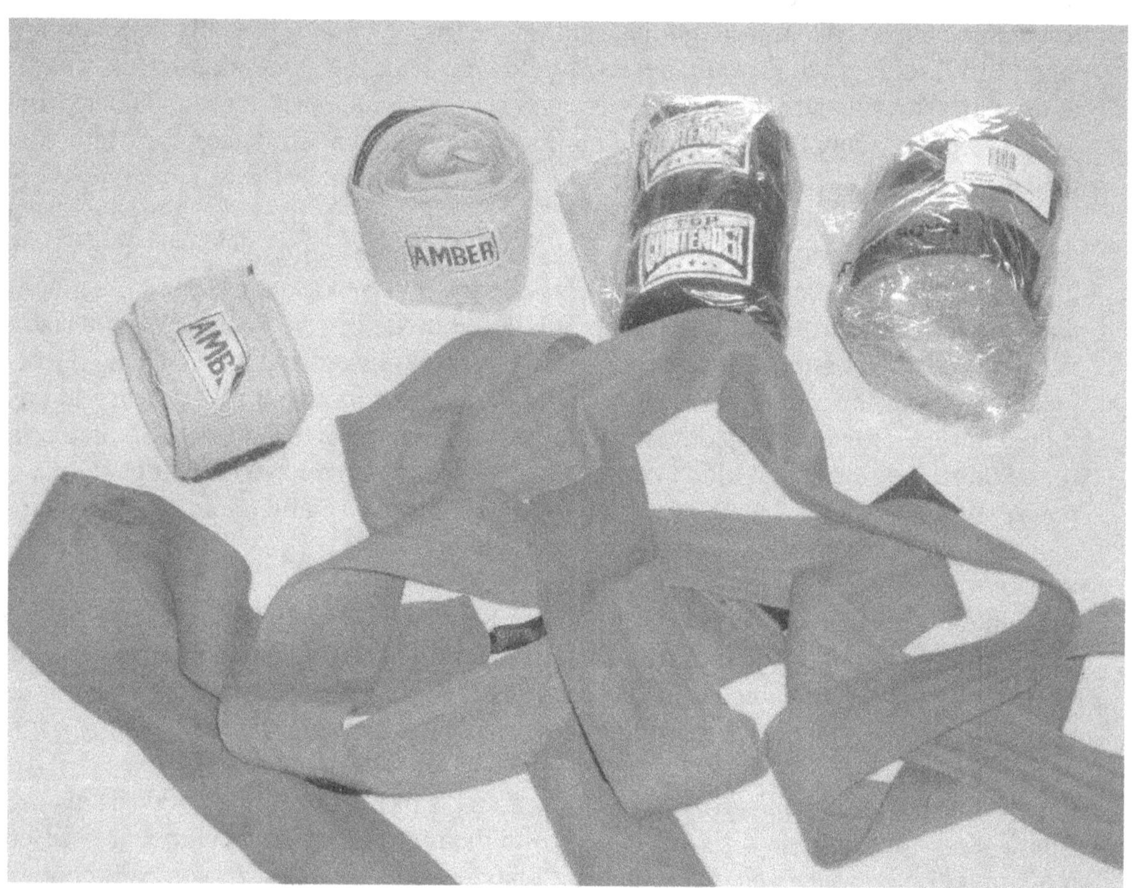

This is one of many ways to wrap your hands. This example is one of the simplest ways to wrap your hands. Wrap your hands snugly. If your hands start turning color or going numb, then you have the wraps too tight.

There is a note on most hand wraps saying "This side down" so put that side down.

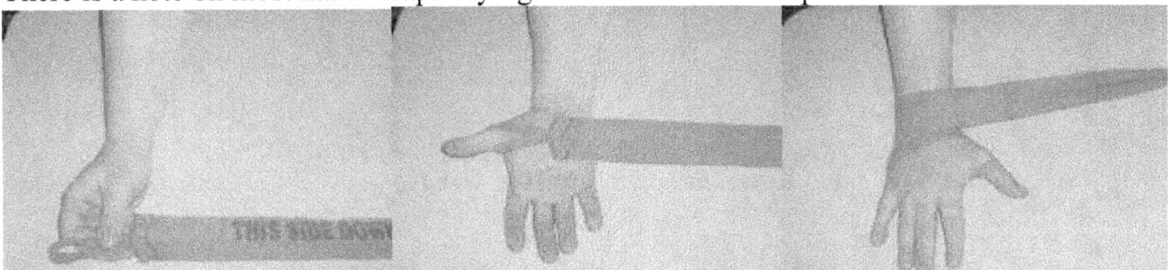

Wrap two times around the wrist then two times around the knuckles

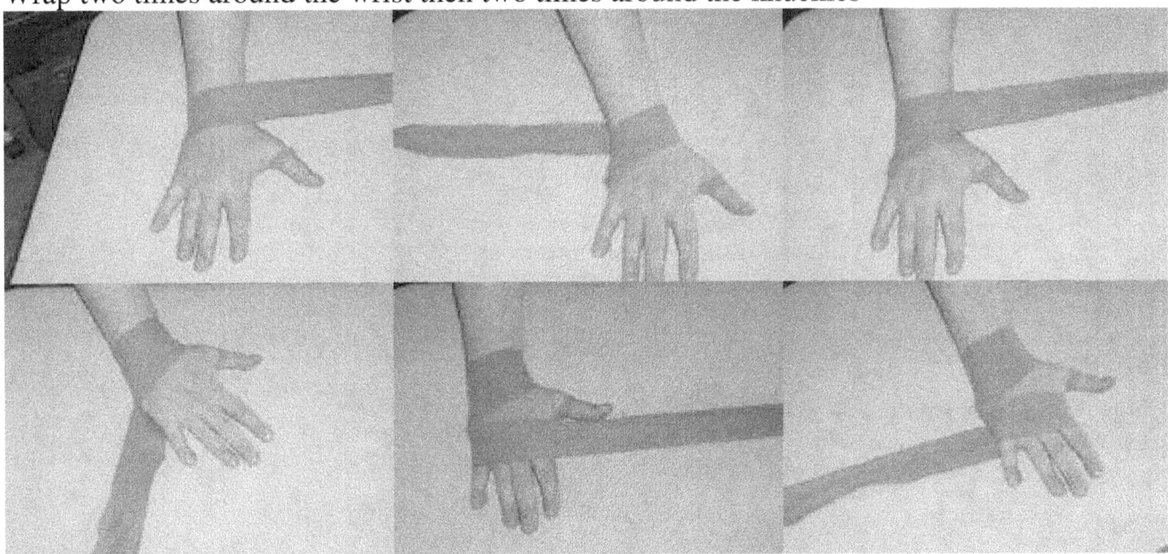

Wrap around the wrist two more times, then straight up between the pointer finger and middle finger.

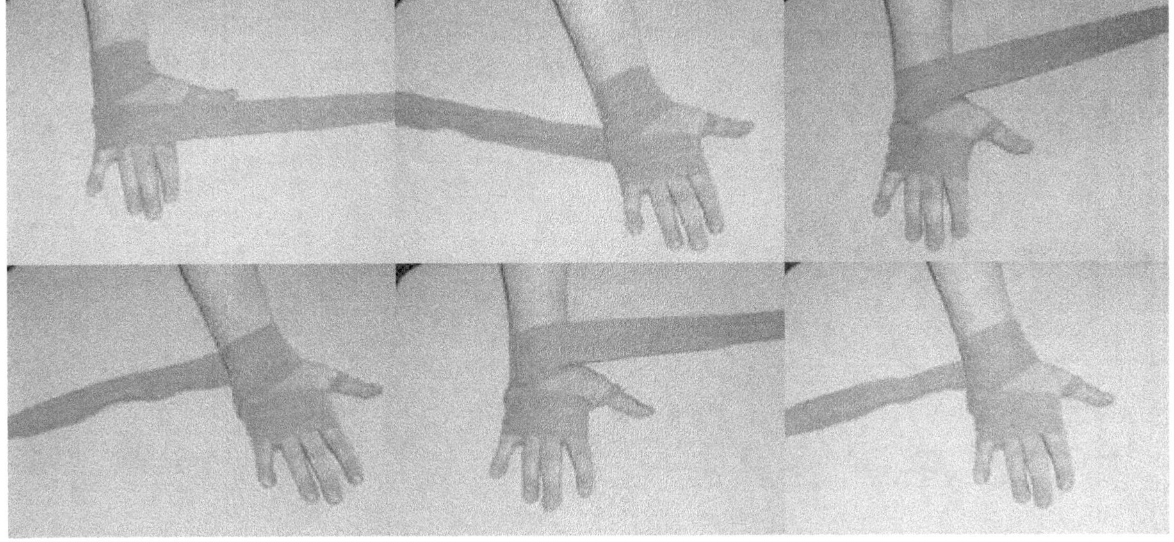

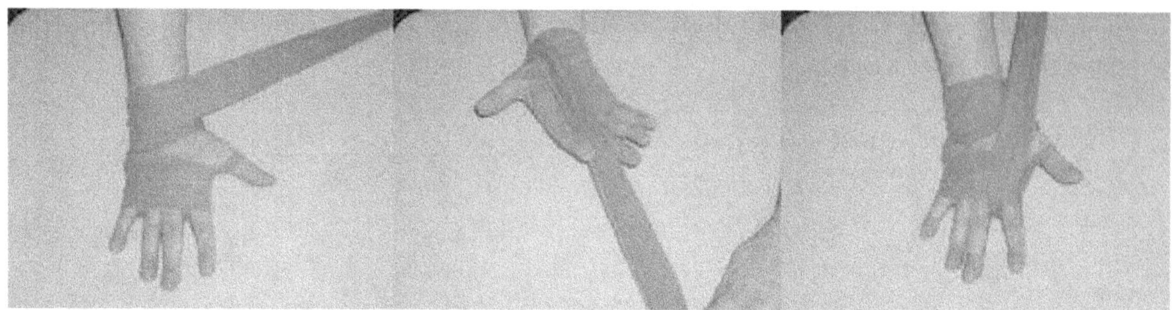

Go back around your thumb and wrap around your wrist twice then around your knuckles two more times.

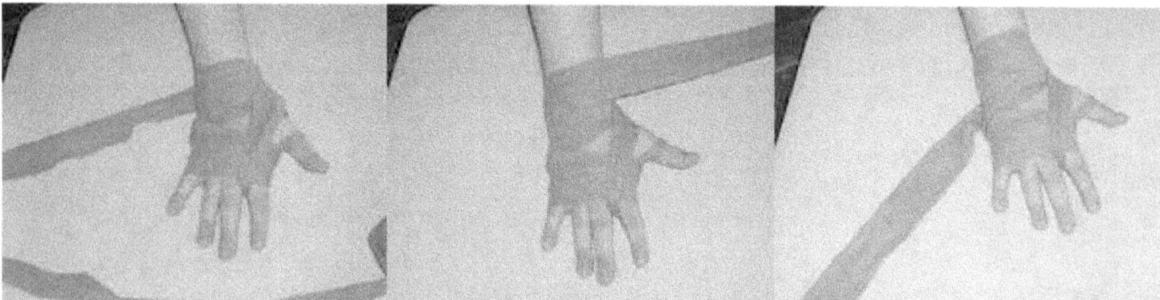

Go crisscross across your hand making an X across the back of the hand. This will help keep the bones in your hand more stable and lessen the likeliness of boxing fracture.

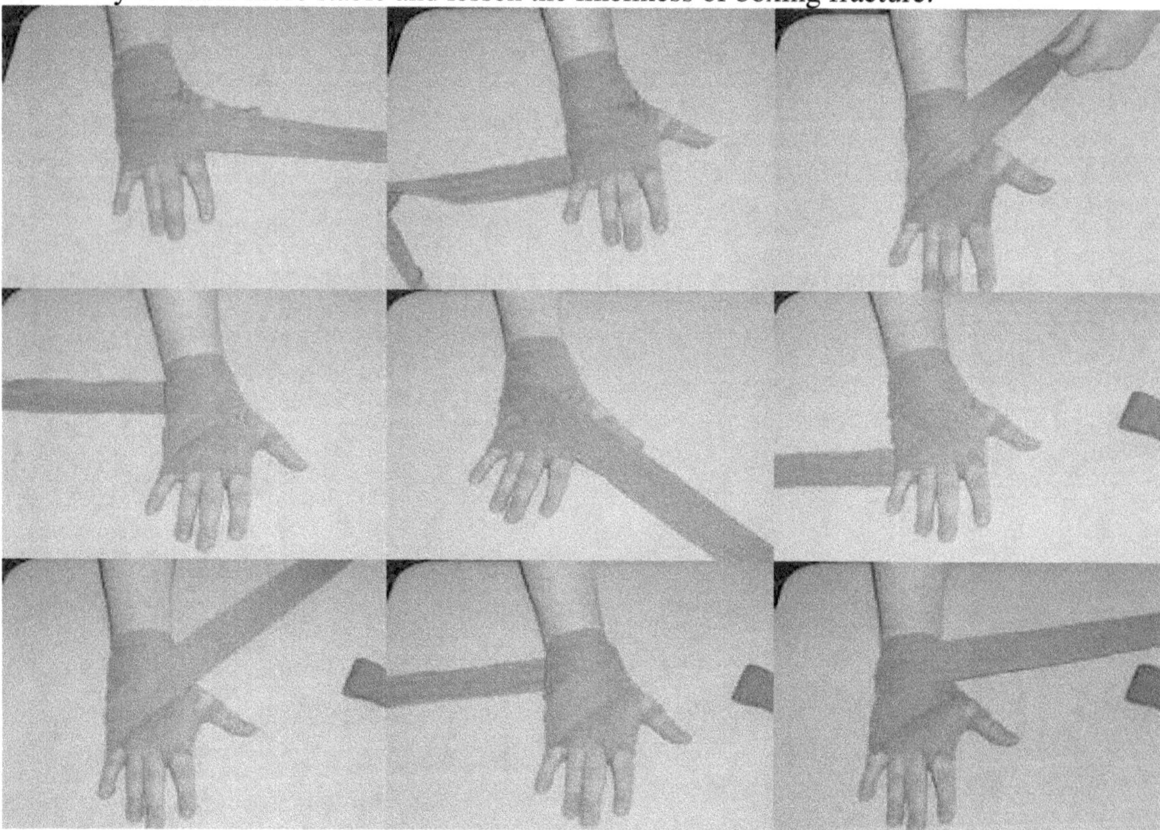

After making your crisscross a couple of times, then go back around your wrist and use up the rest of the length of your wrap.

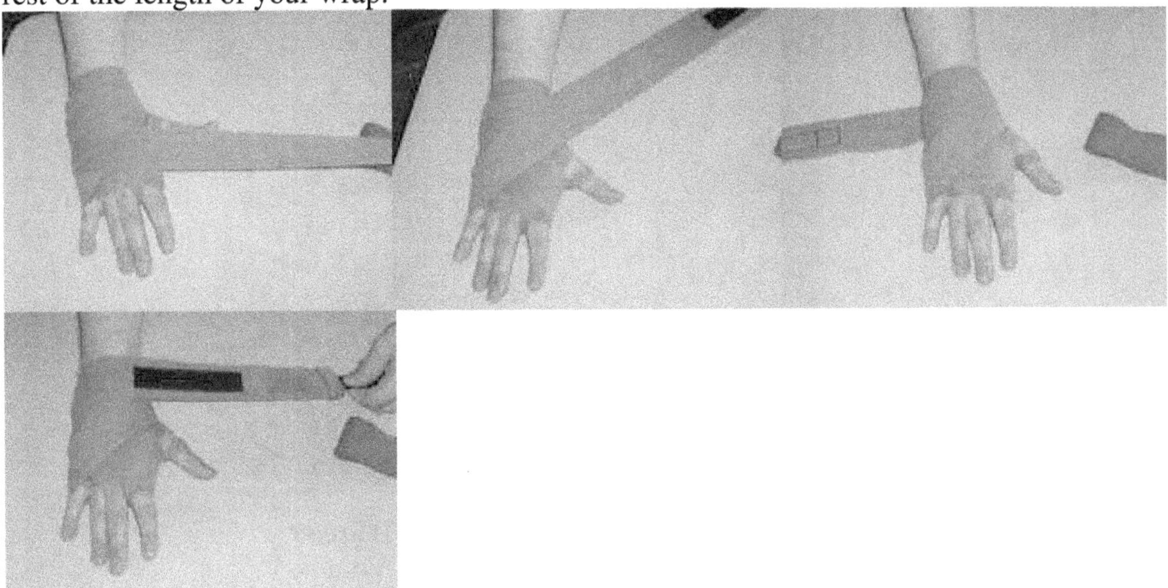

. Books authored by Scott Bolinger
Politics: Last Act of Defiance Volume I
Politics: Last Act of Defiance Volume I (Second Edition)
Politics: Last Act of Defiance Volume II
Politics: Last Act of Defiance Volume III
WarriorRage KickBoxing Volume I
WarriorRage KickBoxing Volume II
WarriorRage KickBoxing Master Edition
Bolinger KickBoxing
Bolinger Boxing (Four Levels of Boxing)
Stretching by Scott Bolinger
Weight Lifting by Scott Bolinger
Boxing Level 1 by Scott Bolinger
Boxing Level 2 by   Scott Bolinger
Boxing Level 3 and 4 by Scott Bolinger
National Self-Defense Solutions
Officials Training Book For Combat Sports
Property Management by Scott Bolinger
Barker Family History

Scott Bolinger

Email: LB@LarryBolinger.com
Website: www. ScottBolinger.website
Facebook: facebook.com/groups/WarriorRage/

Revised 2005
Revised 2009
Revised 2017
Revised 2024